SALAD COOKBOOK
to write in

Belongs to

....

....

....

The Salad Cookbook to Write In is one of the eight recipe books published as part of a larger collection designed to help you write your own recipes in one place and have them at hand when you cook your favorite meals.

This **Special Collection** also includes:

- **SOUPS**
- **PASTRIES**
- **APPETIZERS**
- **DIET RECIPES**
- **OVEN RECIPES**
- **VEGAN RECIPES**
- **CAKES AND PIES**

Table of Contents

Recipe	Page

Table of Contents

Recipe	Page

Table of Contents

Recipe	Page

Table of Contents

Recipe	Page

Table of Contents

Recipe	Page

Recipe:____

Prep time:________   Cook time:________   Servings:________

Ingredients

Directions

Notes

Recipe:____ 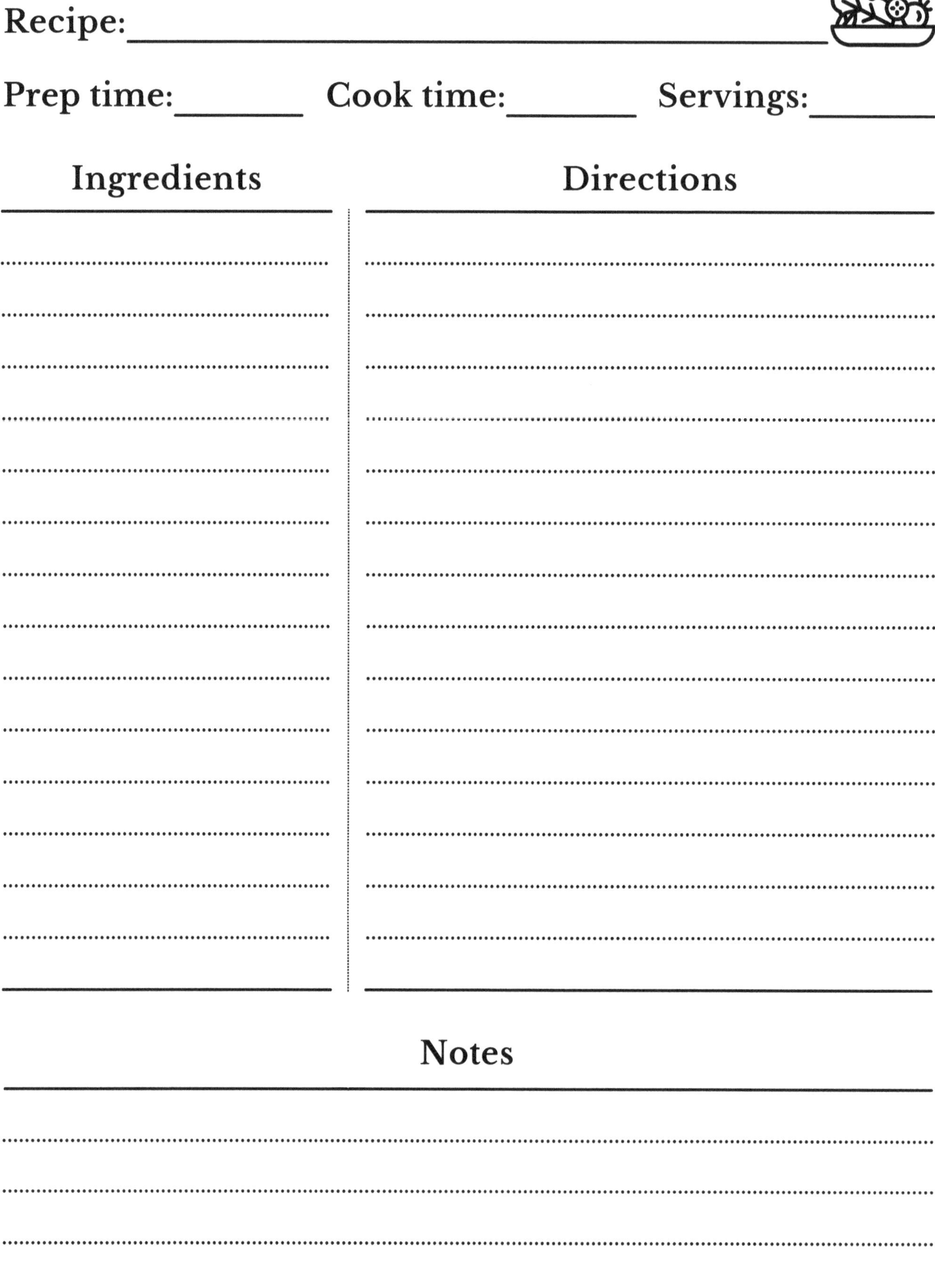

Prep time:_______ Cook time:_______ Servings:_______

Ingredients

Directions

Notes

Recipe: __________________________

Prep time: ______ **Cook time:** ______ **Servings:** ______

Ingredients

Directions

Notes

Recipe:_______________________________________ 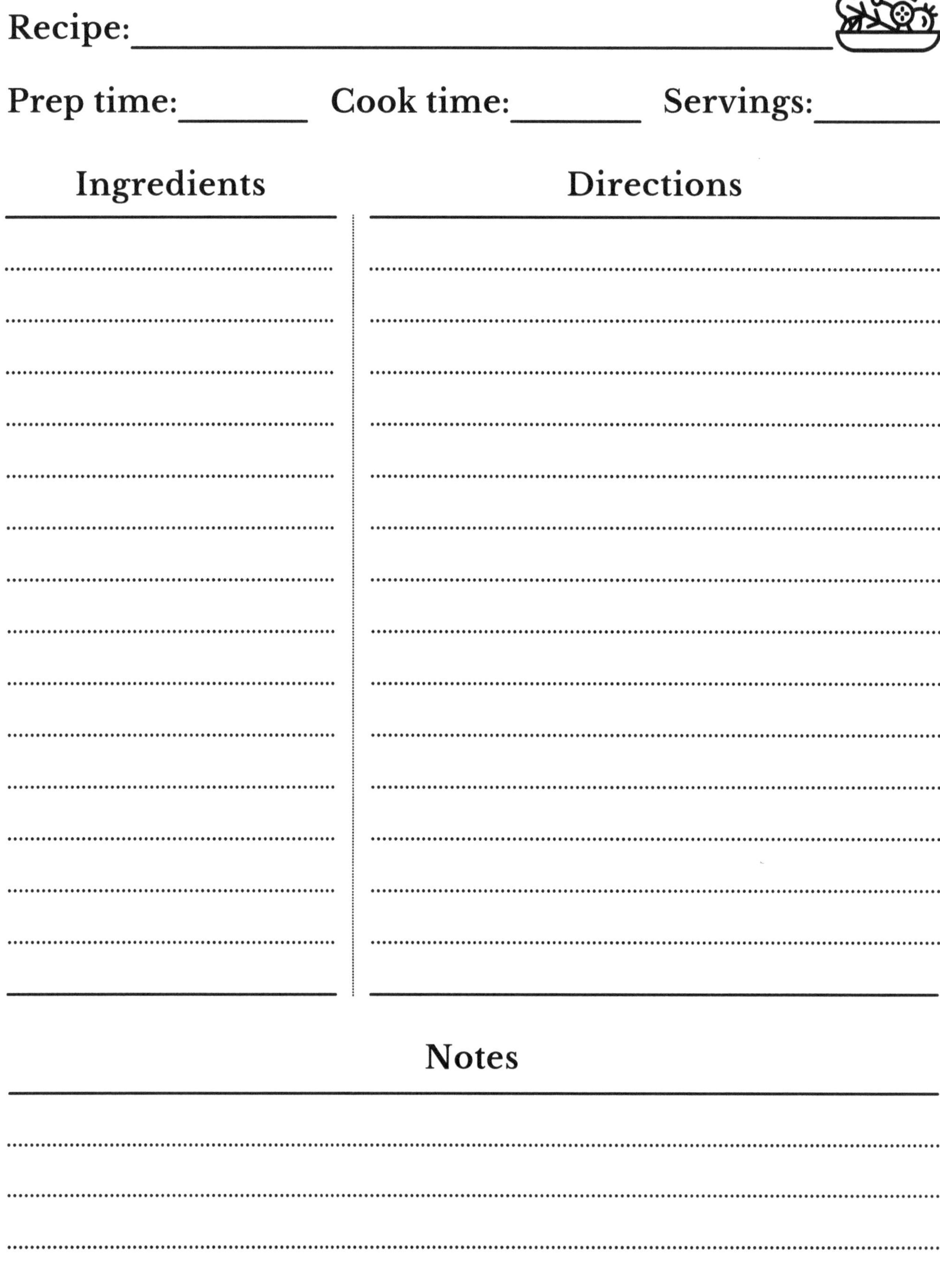

Prep time:________ **Cook time:**________ **Servings:**________

Ingredients	Directions

Notes

Recipe: ______________________________

Prep time: ______ Cook time: ______ Servings: ______

Ingredients	Directions

Notes

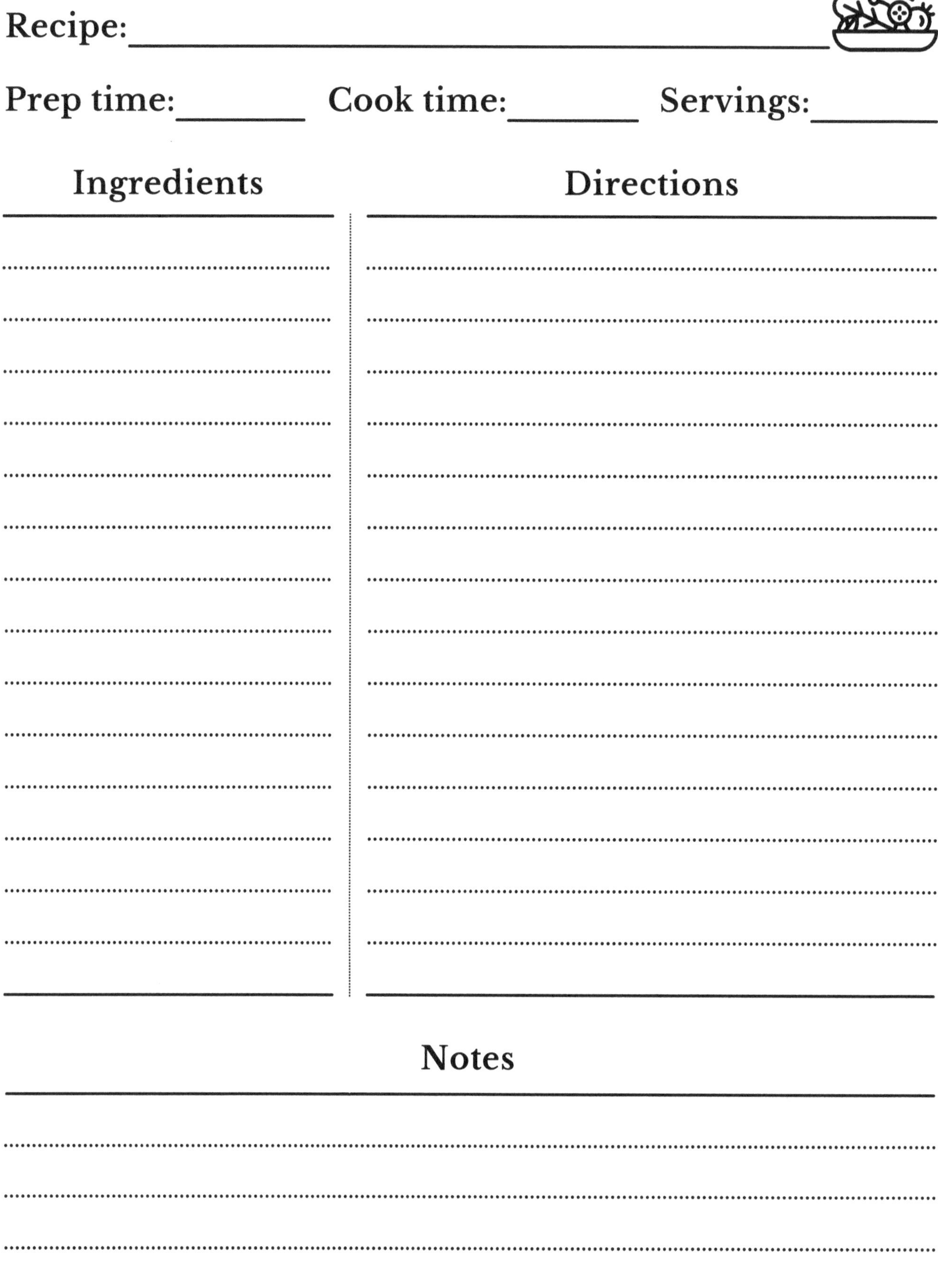

Recipe:____

Prep time:_________ Cook time:_________ Servings:_________

Ingredients

Directions

Notes

Recipe:_______________________________________

Prep time:________ Cook time:________ Servings:________

Ingredients

Directions

Notes

Recipe:____ 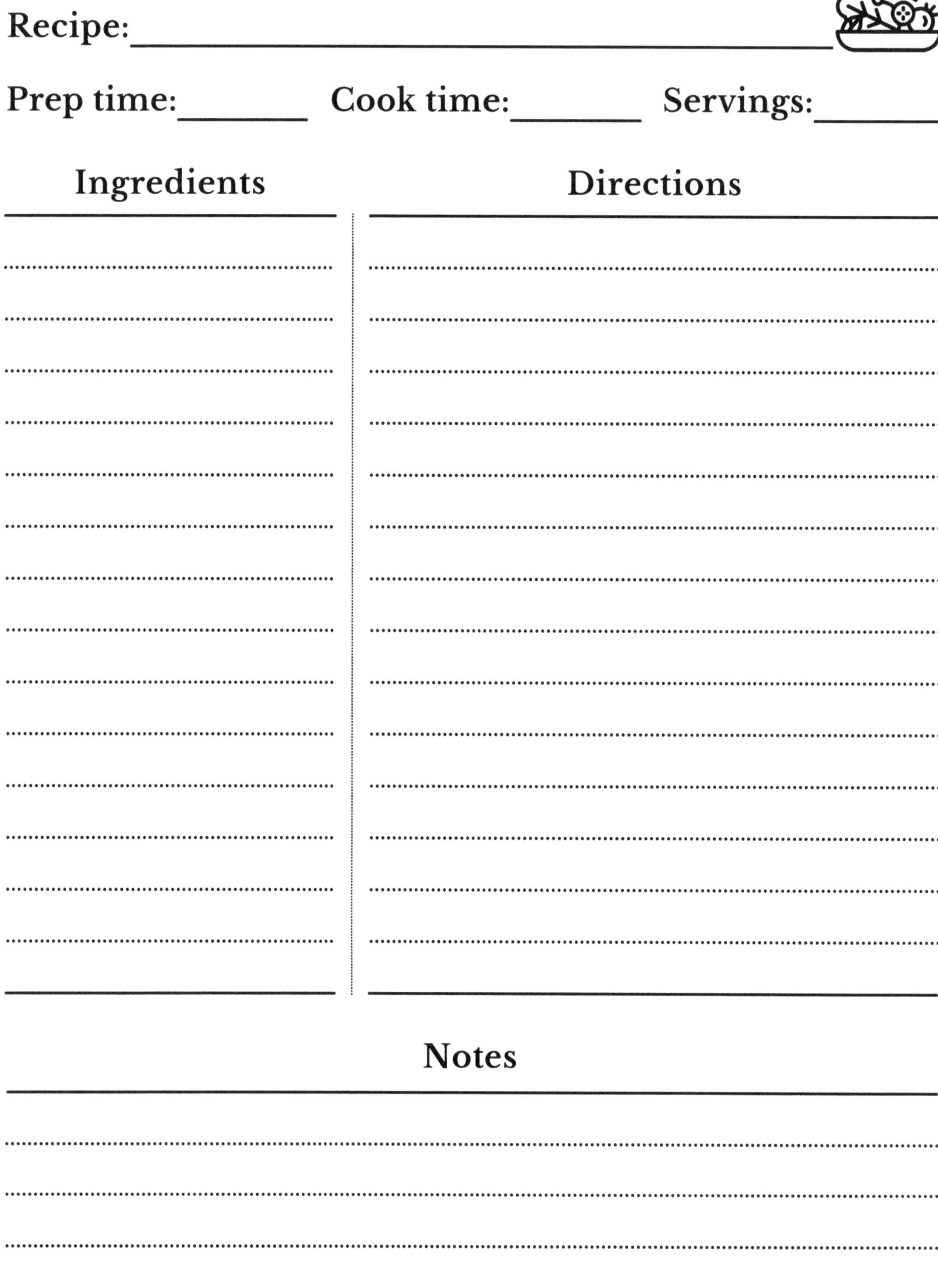

Prep time:_________ **Cook time:**_________ **Servings:**_________

Ingredients | Directions

Notes

Recipe:____

Prep time:_______   Cook time:_______   Servings:_______

Ingredients

Directions

Notes

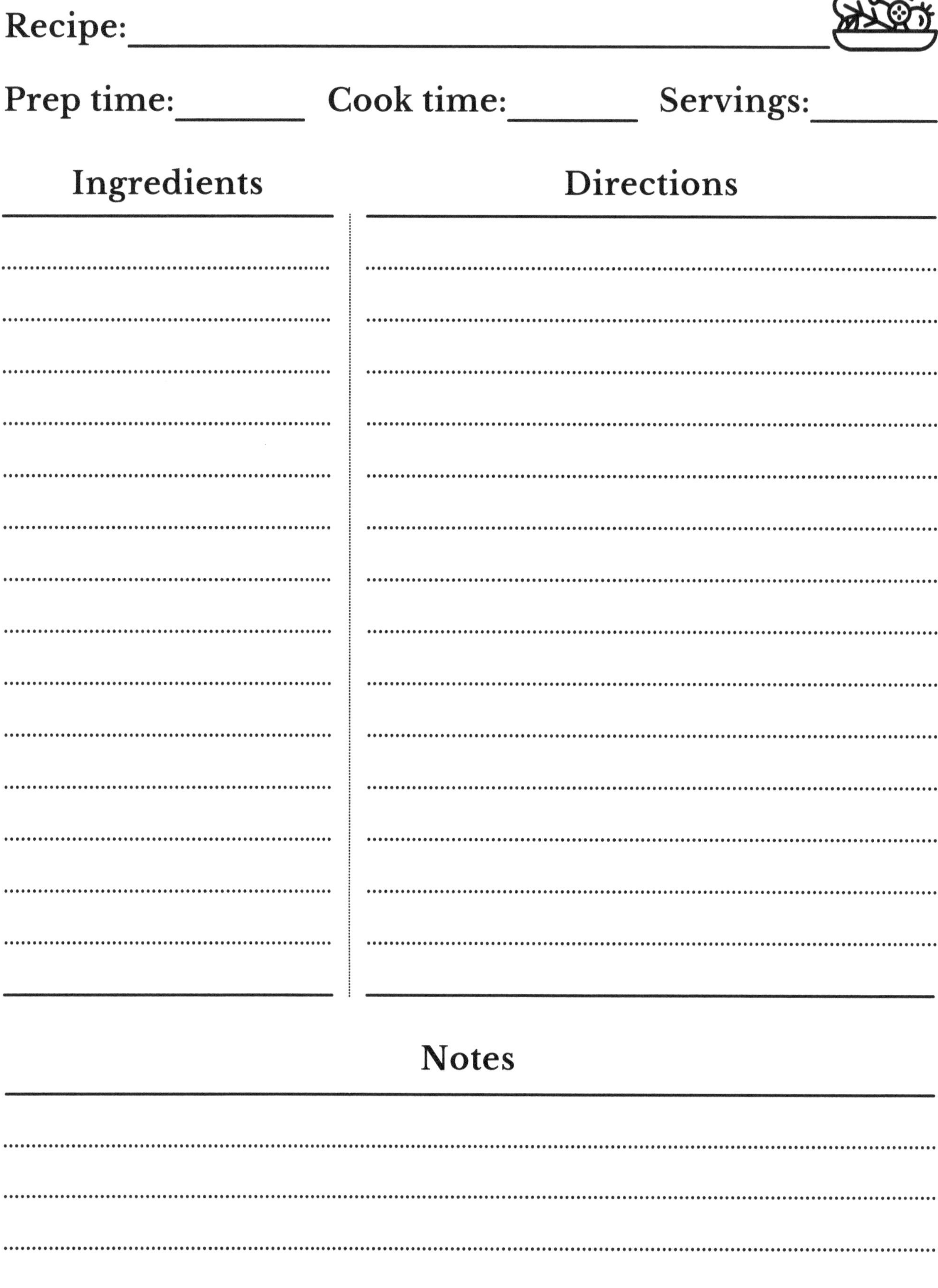

Recipe:

Prep time:______   Cook time:______   Servings:______

Ingredients

Directions

Notes

Recipe:_______________________________________ 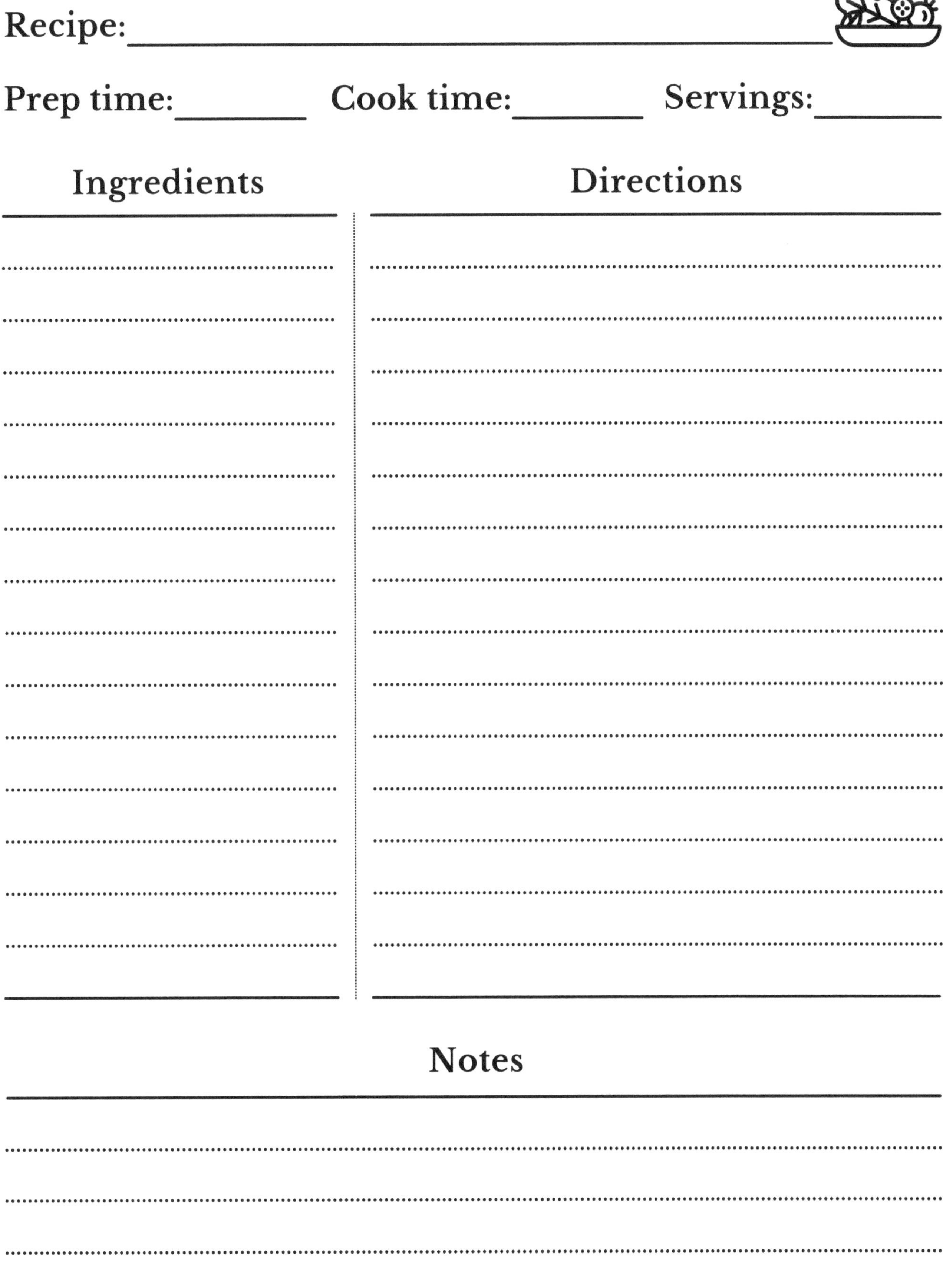

Prep time:______   Cook time:______   Servings:______

Ingredients	Directions

Notes

Recipe:____

Prep time:________   Cook time:________   Servings:________

Ingredients

Directions

Notes

Recipe:_______________________________

Prep time:________   Cook time:________   Servings:________

Ingredients

Directions

Notes

Recipe:____ 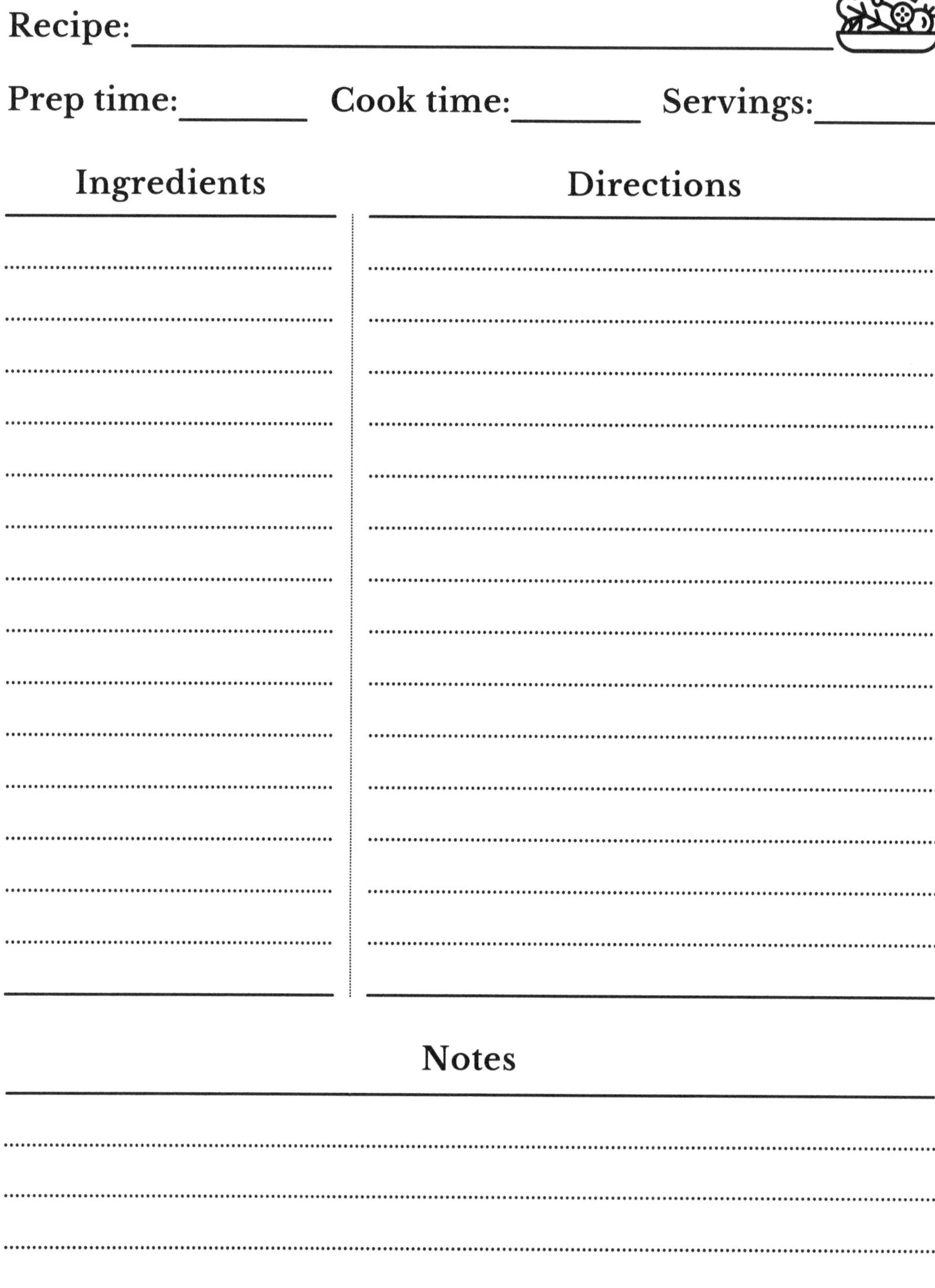

Prep time:_______ Cook time:_______ Servings:_______

Ingredients

Directions

Notes

Recipe:____ 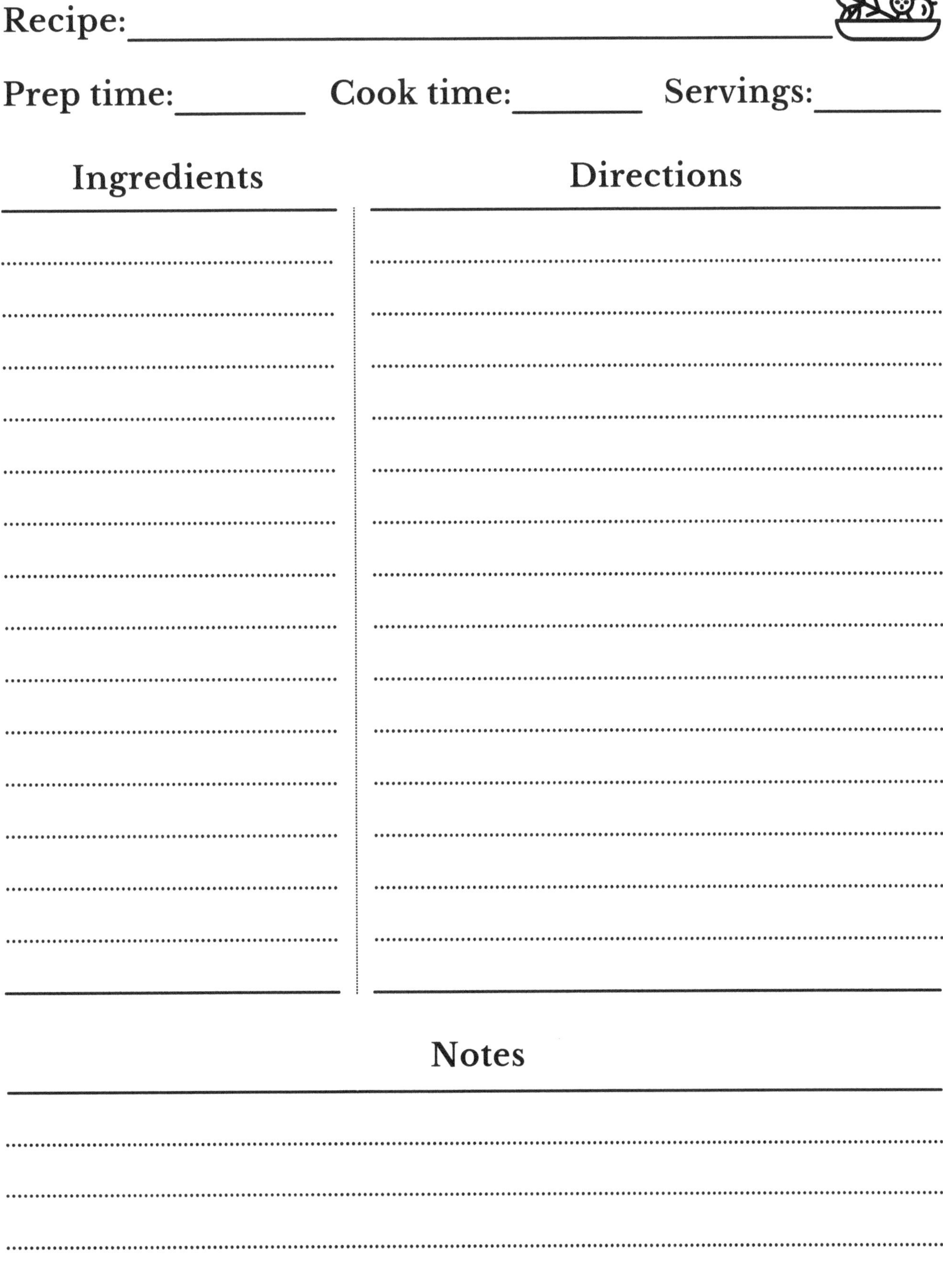

Prep time:_______   Cook time:_______   Servings:_______

Ingredients

Directions

Notes

Recipe:____

Prep time:_______   Cook time:_______   Servings:_______

Ingredients

Directions

Notes

Recipe:____

Prep time:_______   Cook time:_______   Servings:_______

Ingredients | ## Directions

Notes

Recipe:____ 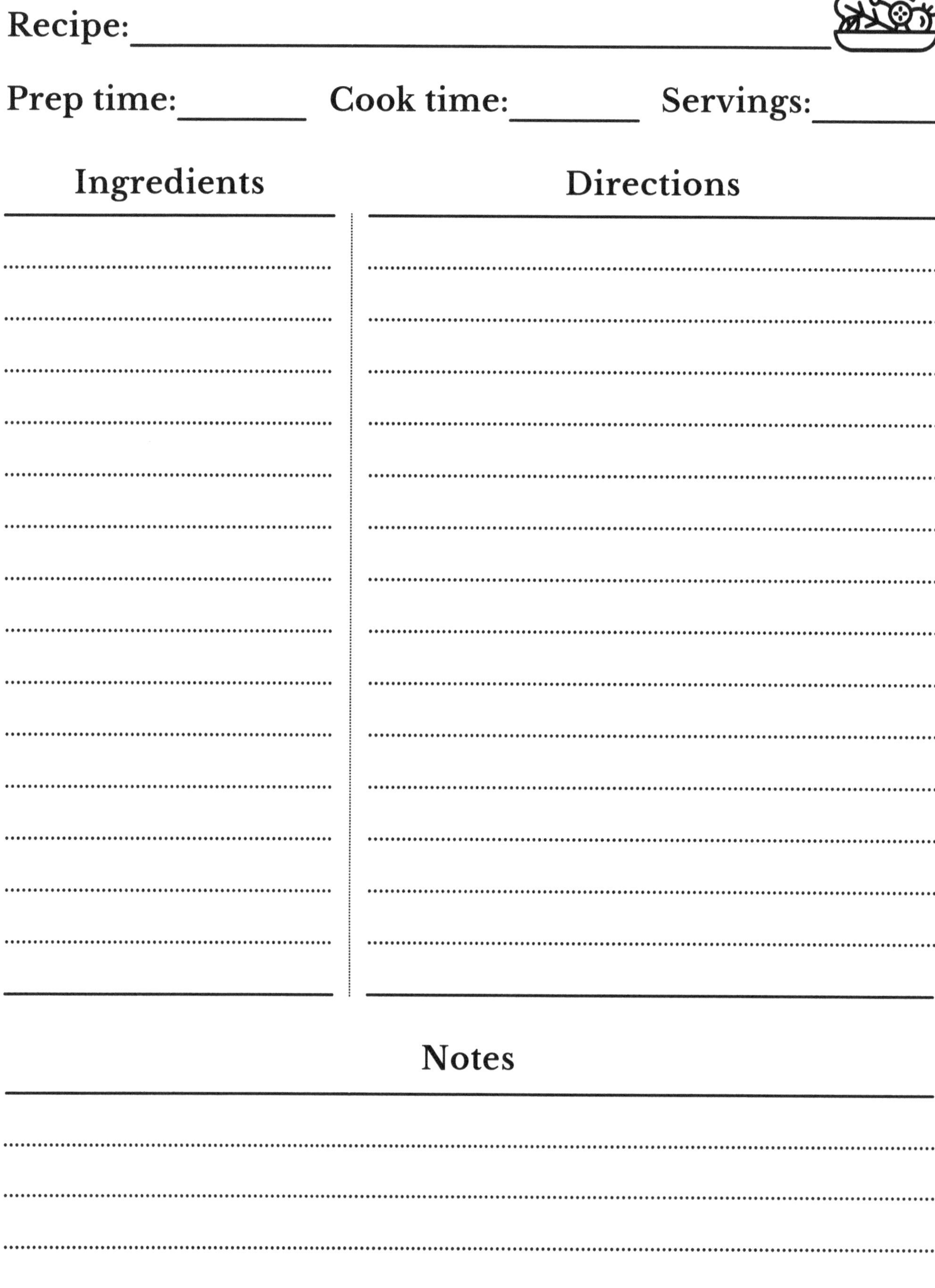

Prep time:________   Cook time:________   Servings:________

| Ingredients | Directions |

Notes

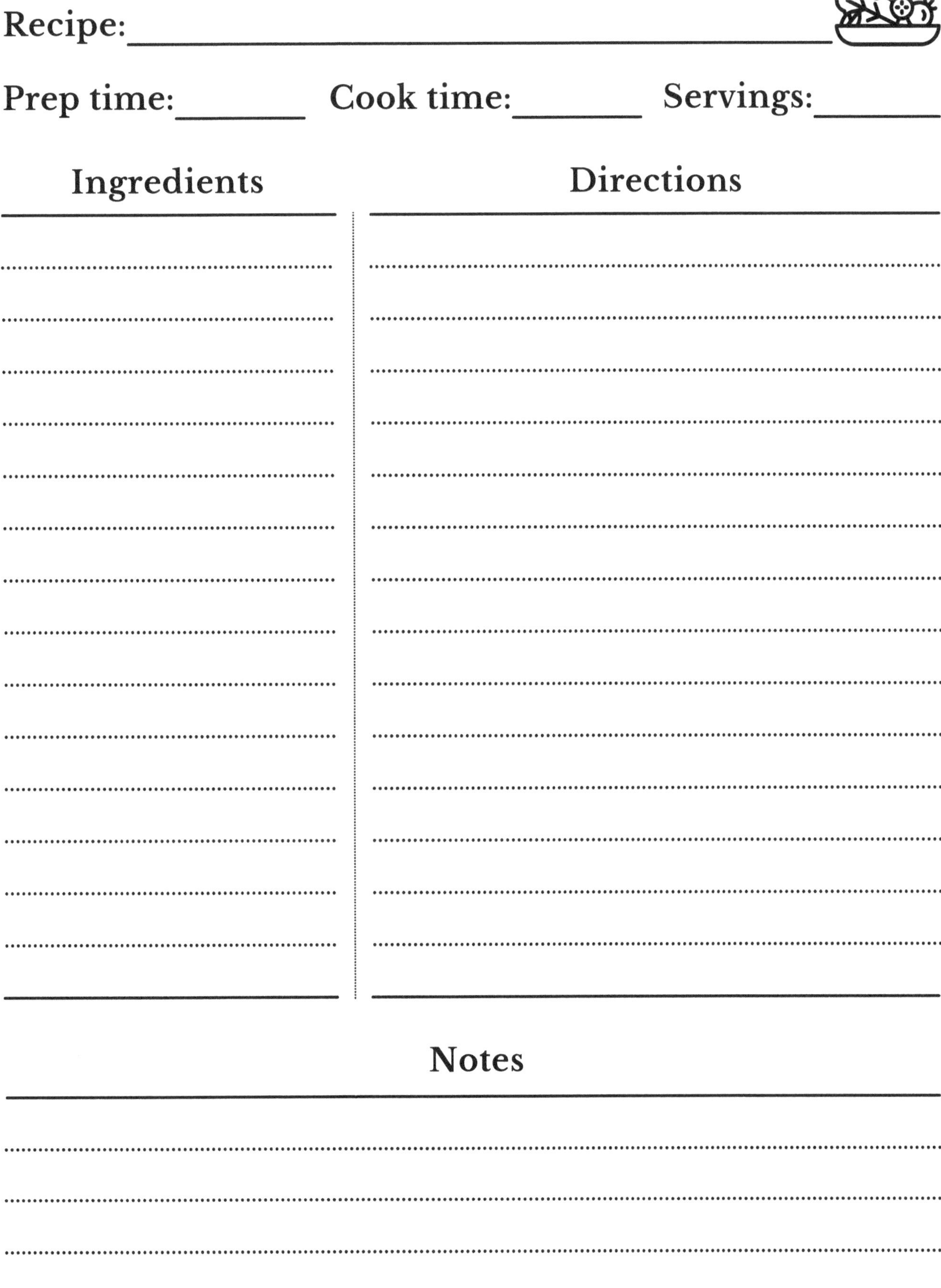

Recipe:_______________________________

Prep time:______ Cook time:______ Servings:______

Ingredients

Directions

Notes

Recipe:

Prep time: _______ Cook time: _______ Servings: _______

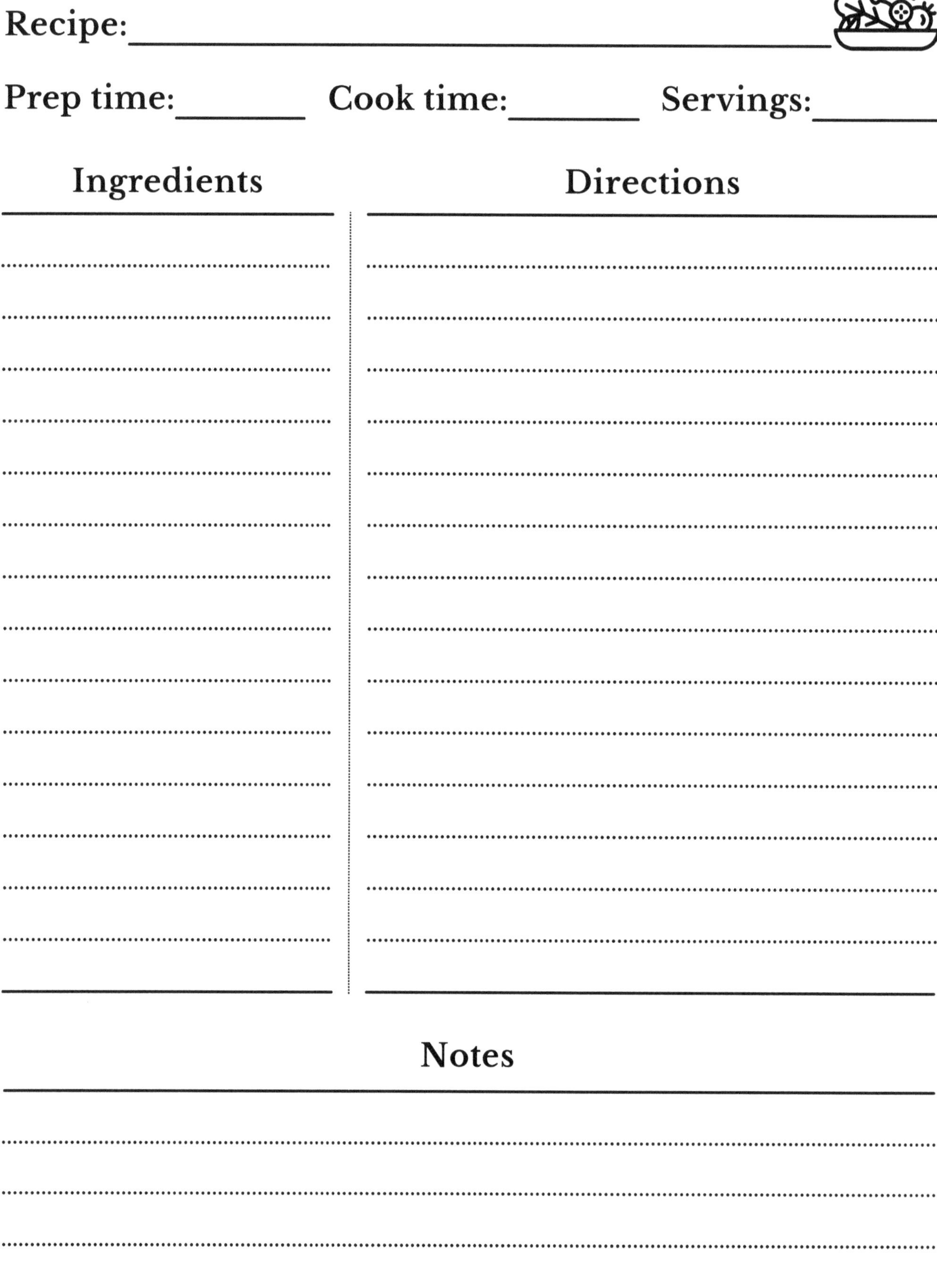

Ingredients

Directions

Notes

Recipe:____

Prep time:______   Cook time:______   Servings:______

Ingredients

Directions

Notes

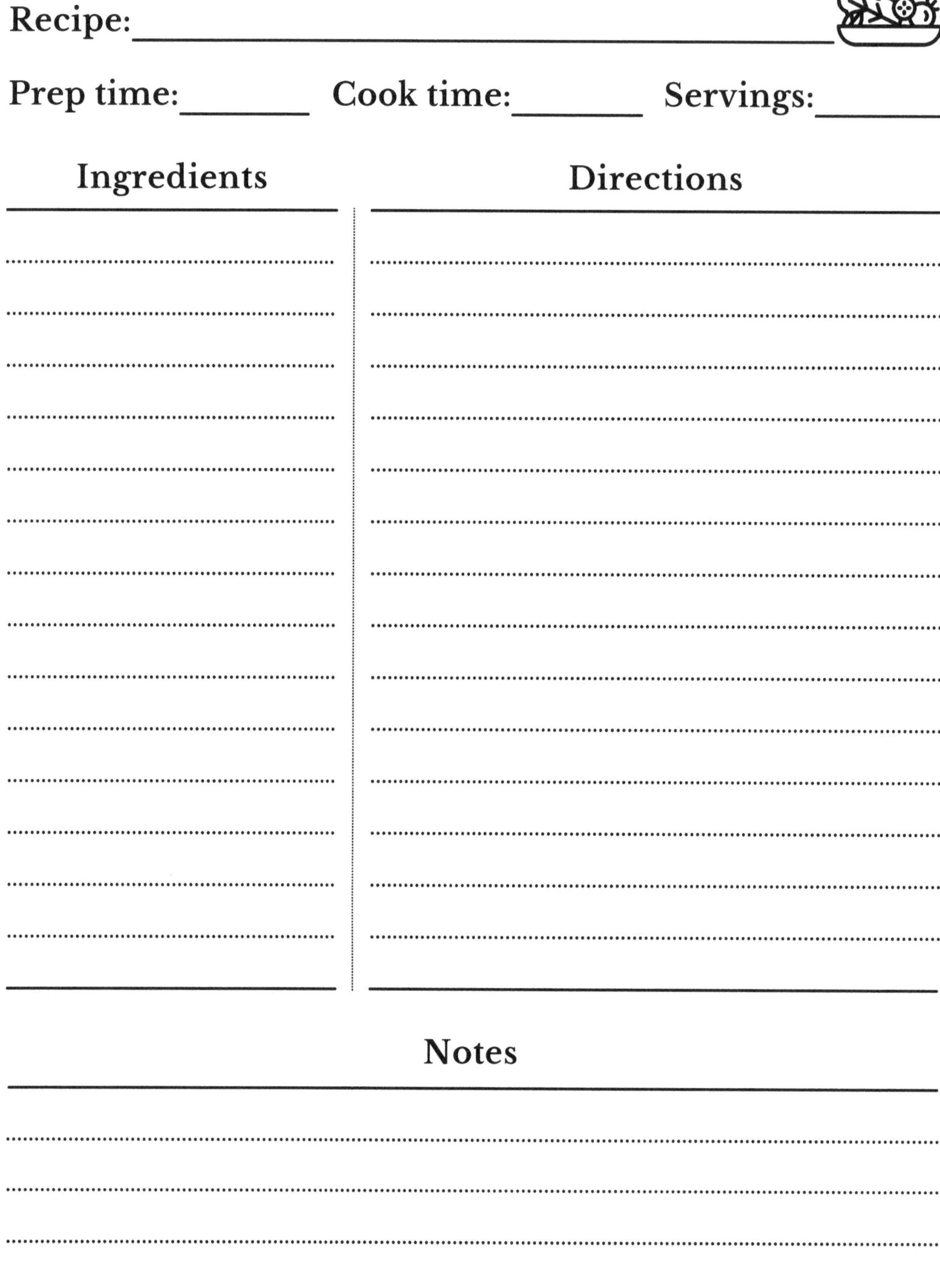

Recipe:

Prep time: ______   **Cook time:** ______   **Servings:** ______

Ingredients

Directions

Notes

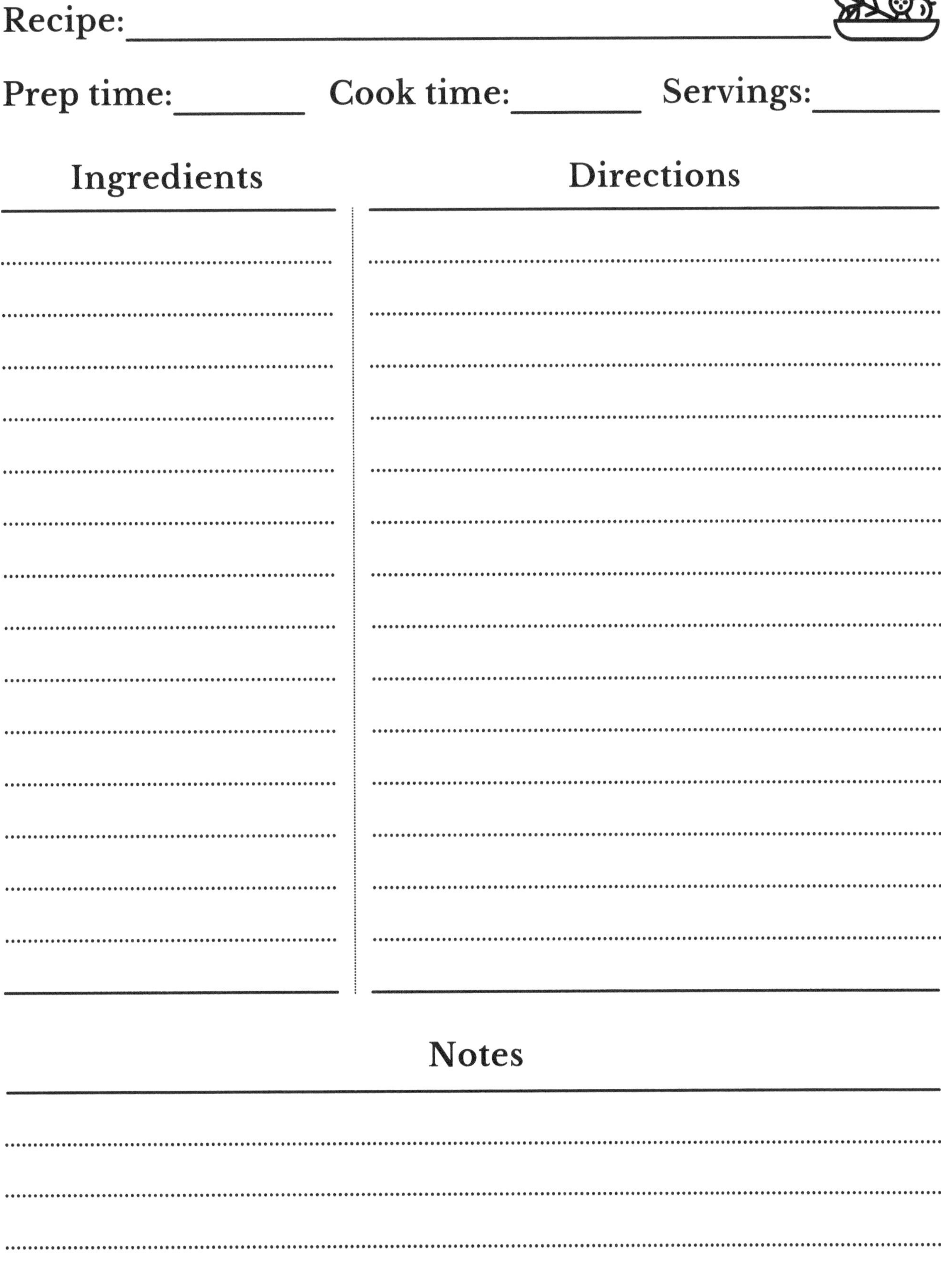

Recipe:____

Prep time:_______ Cook time:_______ Servings:_______

Ingredients

Directions

Notes

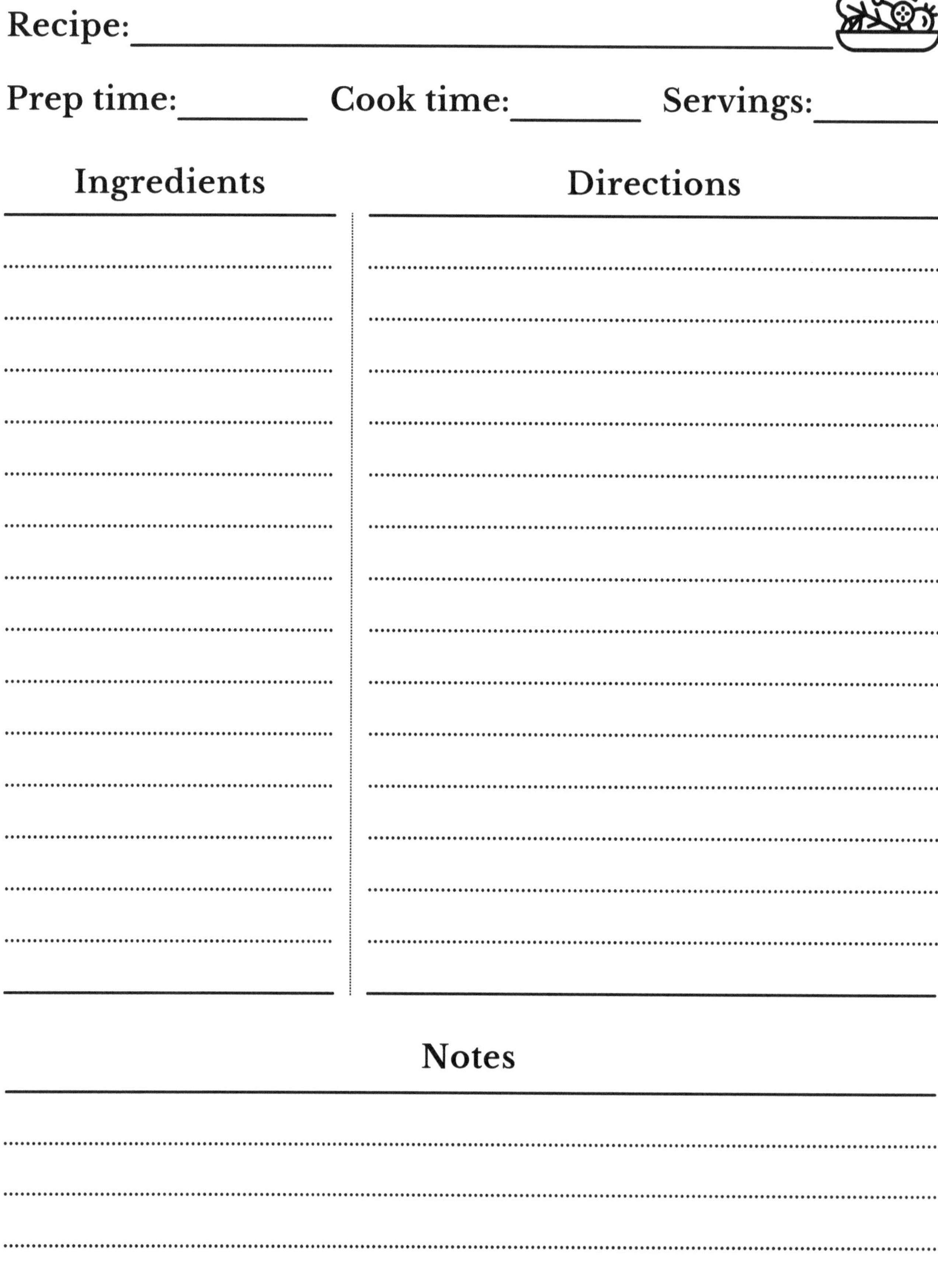

Recipe:

Prep time:______ **Cook time:**______ **Servings:**______

Ingredients

Directions

Notes

Recipe:____

Prep time:_______   Cook time:_______   Servings:_______

Ingredients

Directions

Notes

Recipe:

Prep time: ______ **Cook time:** ______ **Servings:** ______

Ingredients

Directions

Notes

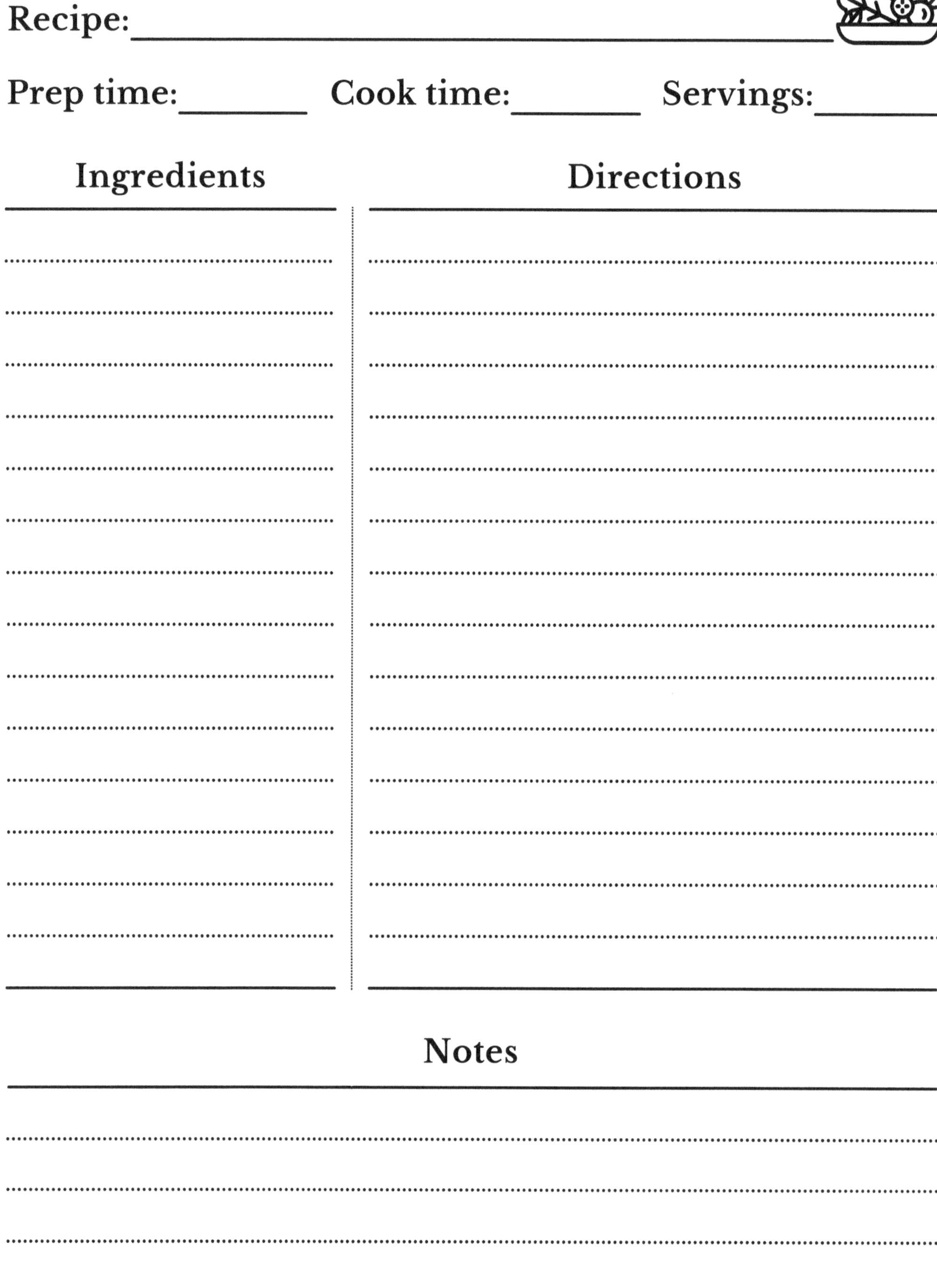

Recipe:____ 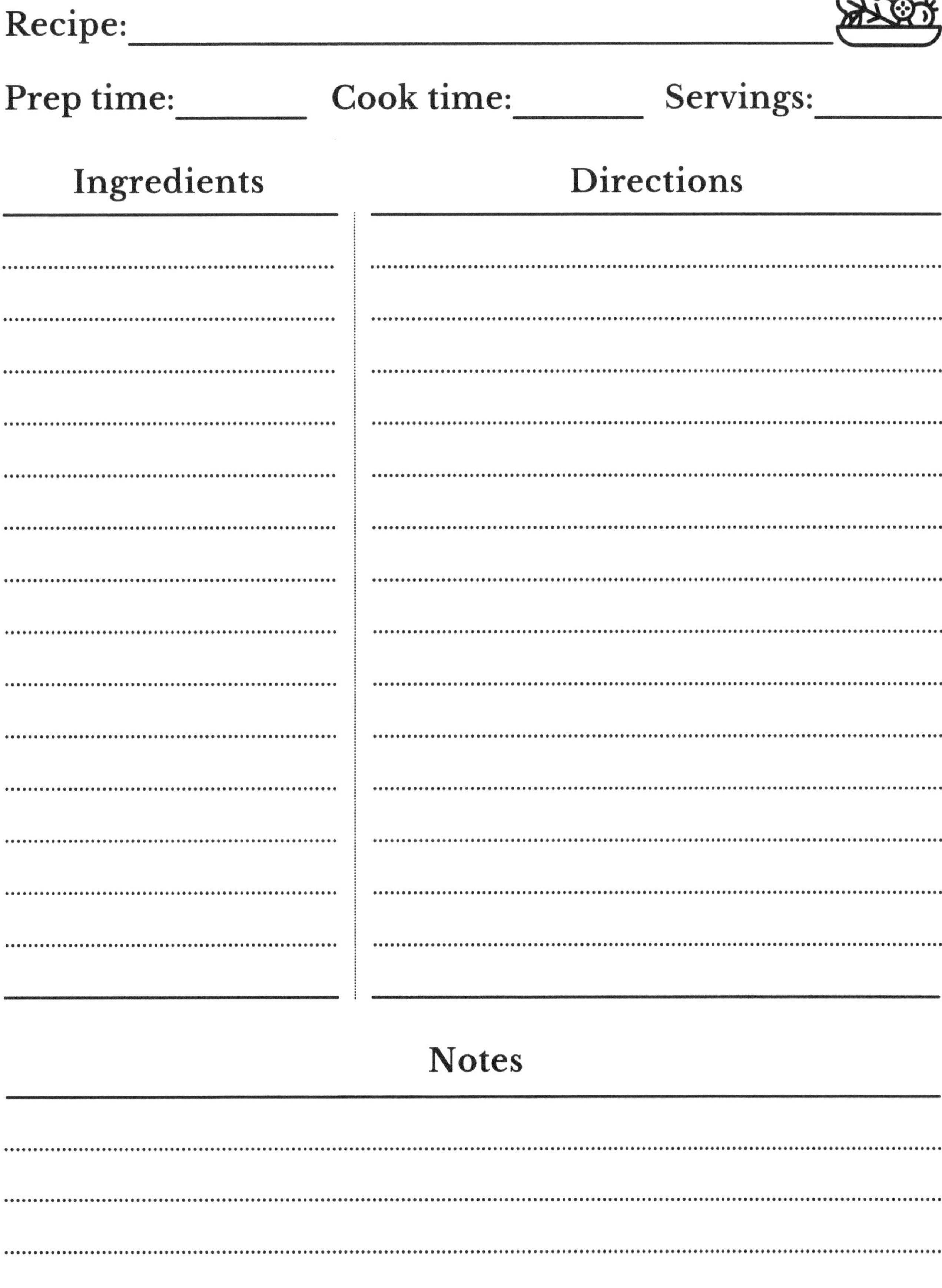

Prep time:______   **Cook time:**______   **Servings:**______

Ingredients

Directions

Notes

Recipe:____

Prep time:________   Cook time:________   Servings:________

Ingredients

Directions

Notes

Recipe:____

Prep time:________   Cook time:________   Servings:________

Ingredients   ## Directions

Notes

Recipe:

Prep time:_______ **Cook time:**_______ **Servings:**_______

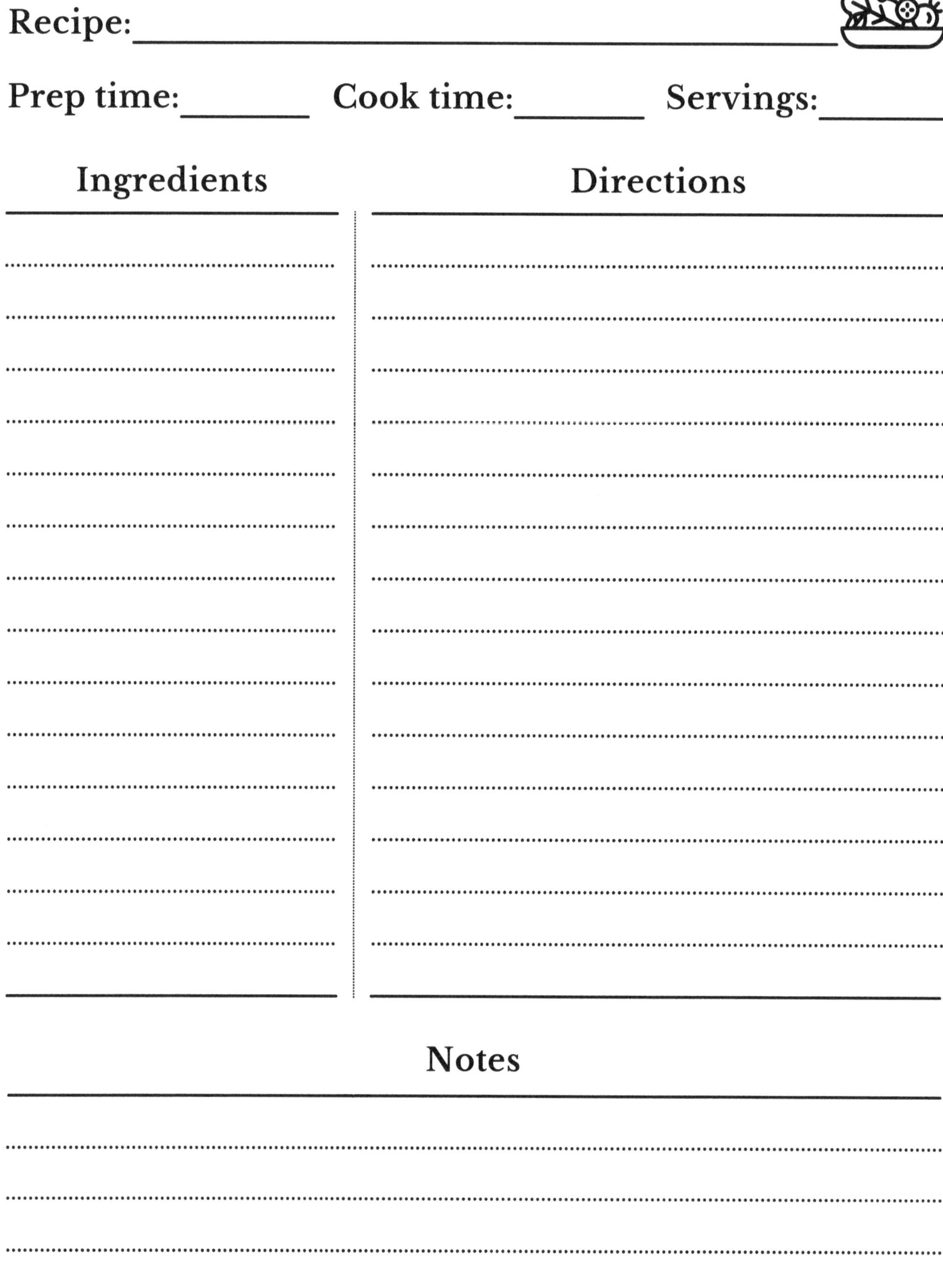

Ingredients	Directions

Notes

Recipe:_______________________________________

Prep time:_______   Cook time:_______   Servings:_______

Ingredients

Directions

Notes

Recipe:____

Prep time:_______   Cook time:_______   Servings:_______

<table>
<tr><td>Ingredients</td><td>Directions</td></tr>
</table>

Notes

Recipe:____

Prep time:________   Cook time:________   Servings:________

Ingredients

Directions

Notes

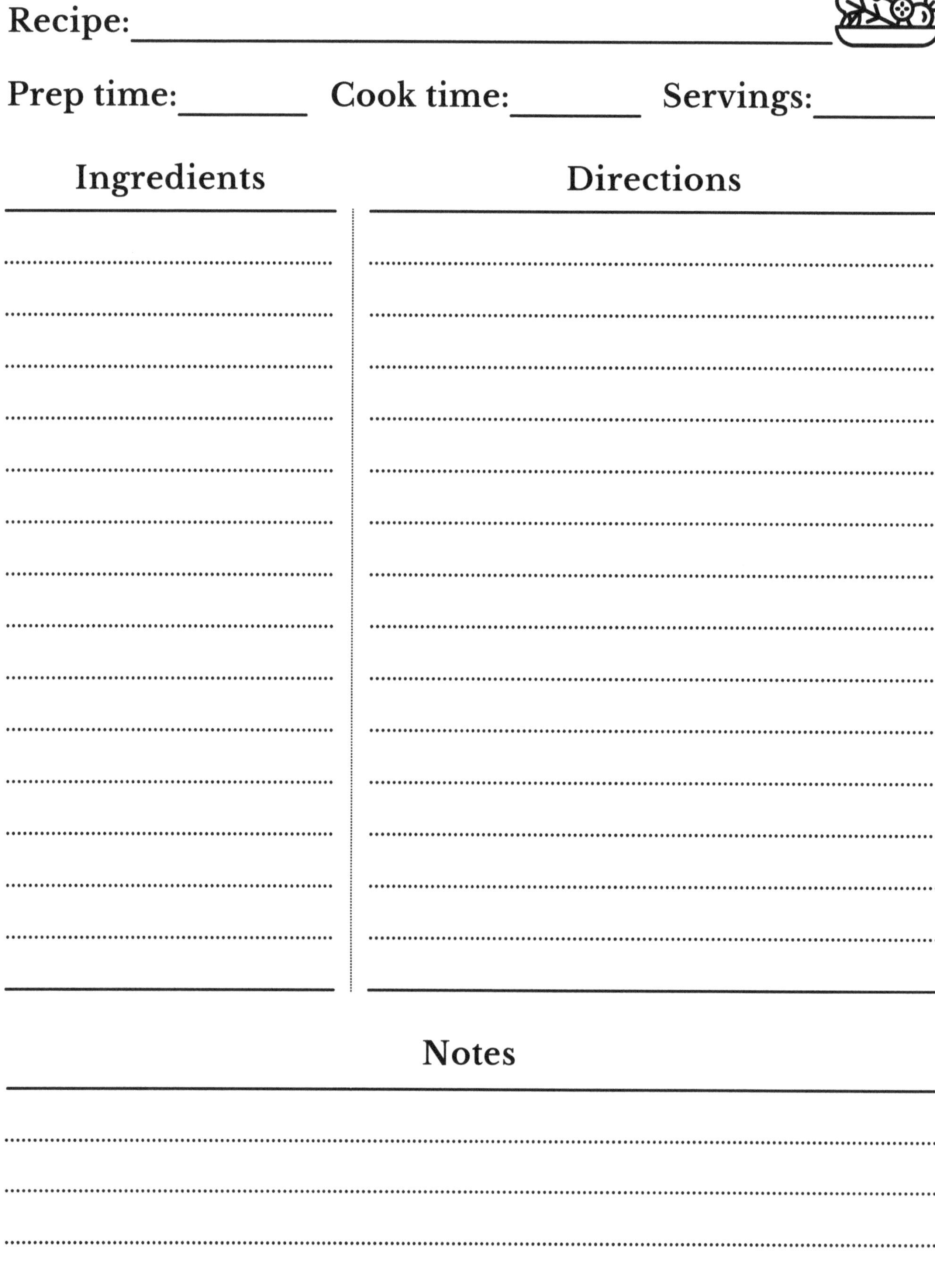

Recipe:____

Prep time:_______ Cook time:_______ Servings:_______

Ingredients

Directions

Notes

Recipe:____

Prep time:_______   Cook time:_______   Servings:_______

Ingredients

Directions

Notes

Recipe:____

Prep time:_________ Cook time:_________ Servings:_________

Ingredients

Directions

Notes

Recipe:____________________________

Prep time:______   Cook time:______   Servings:______

Ingredients

Directions

Notes

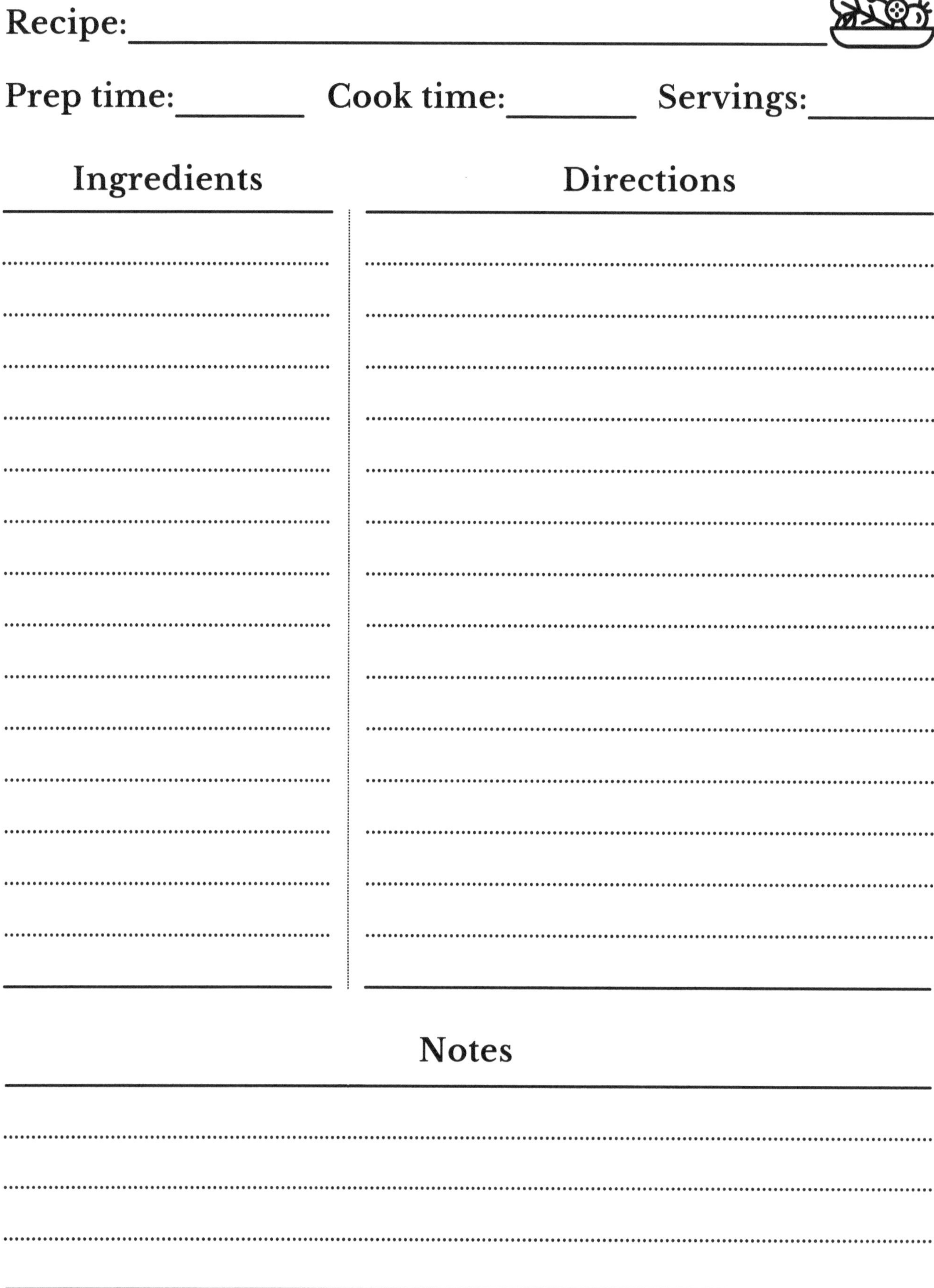

Recipe:________________________________

Prep time:______ **Cook time:**______ **Servings:**______

Ingredients

Directions

Notes

Recipe:____

Prep time:_______   Cook time:_______   Servings:_______

Ingredients

Directions

Notes

Recipe:____

Prep time:________   Cook time:________   Servings:________

Ingredients

Directions

Notes

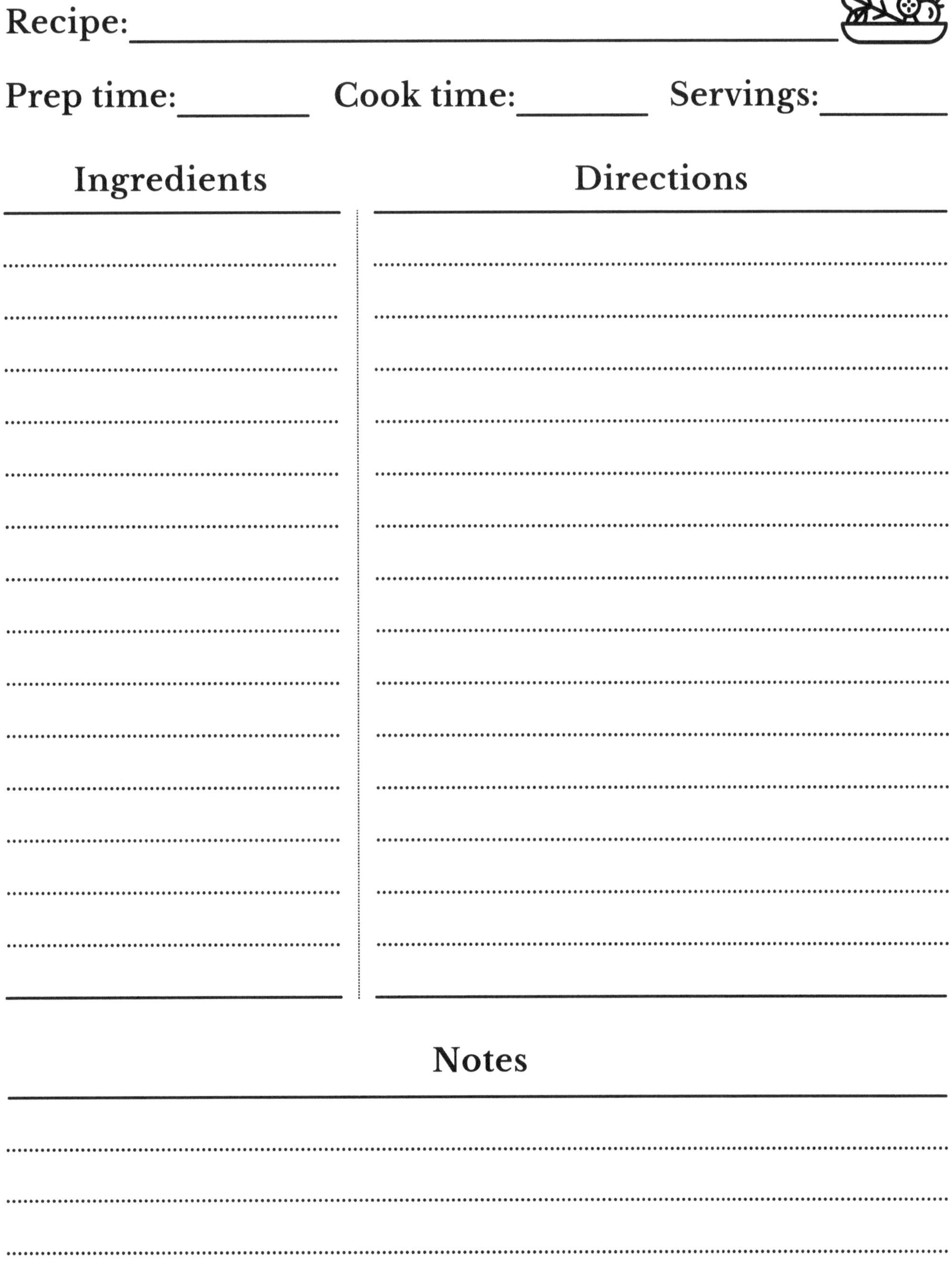

Recipe:____

Prep time:________   Cook time:________   Servings:________

Ingredients

Directions

Notes

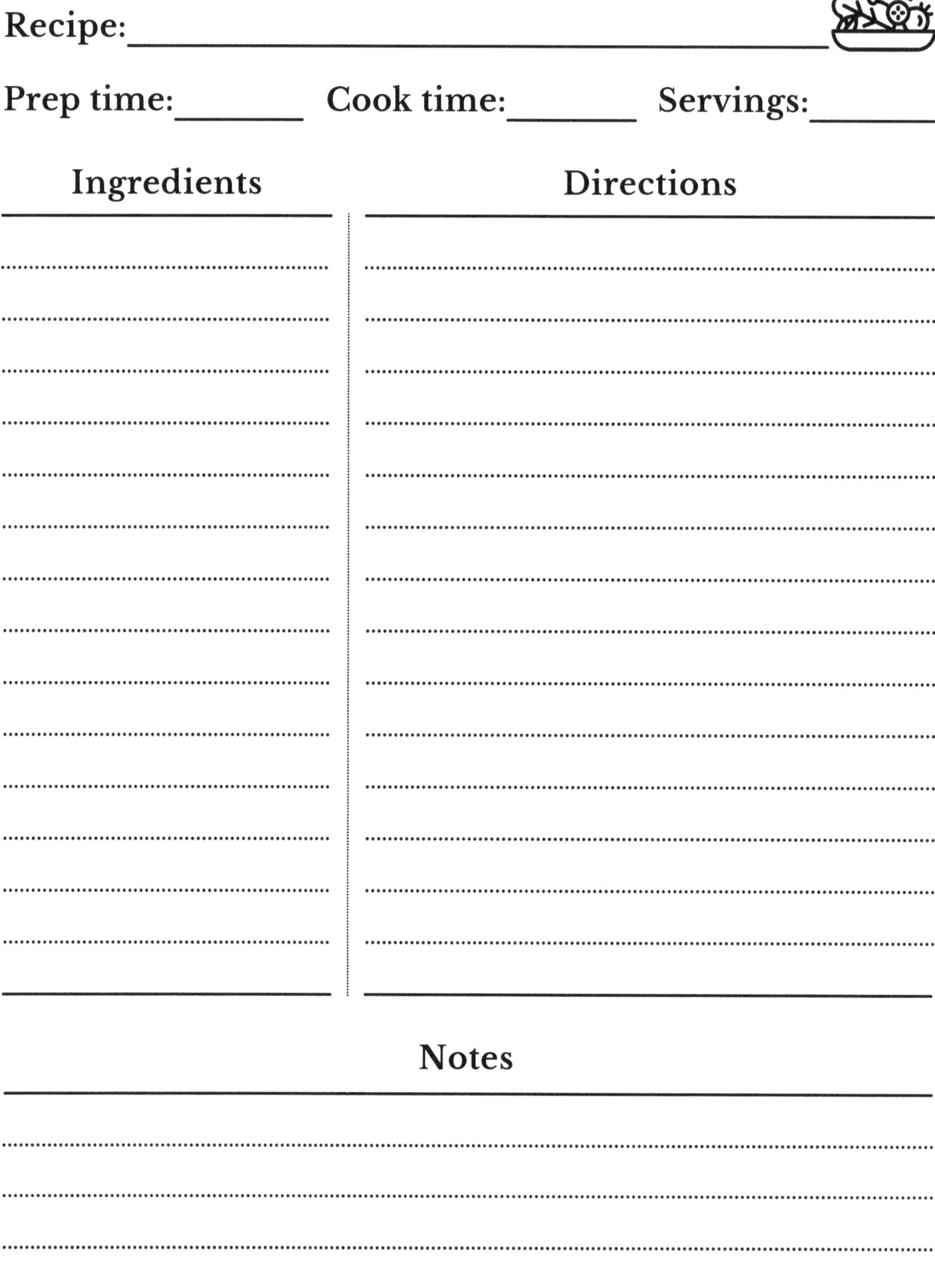

Recipe:

Prep time: _______ **Cook time:** _______ **Servings:** _______

Ingredients

Directions

Notes

Recipe:____

Prep time:________   Cook time:________   Servings:________

Ingredients

Directions

Notes

Recipe:_______________________________

Prep time:________ **Cook time:**________ **Servings:**________

Ingredients

Directions

Notes

Recipe:____

Prep time:_________   Cook time:_________   Servings:_________

| Ingredients | Directions |

Notes

Recipe:____ 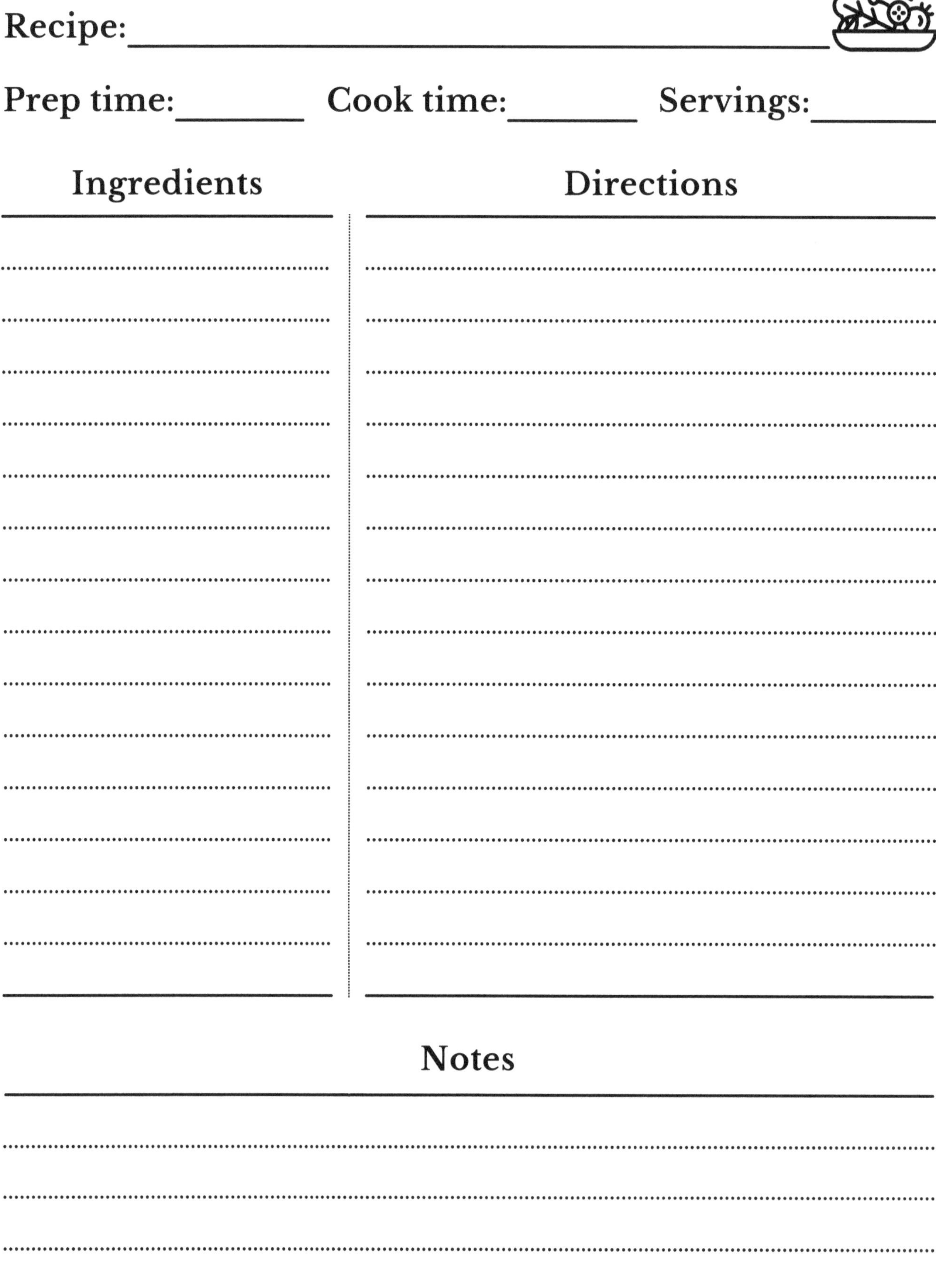

Prep time:_______ **Cook time:**_______ **Servings:**_______

Ingredients

Directions

Notes

Recipe:_______________________________________

Prep time:_______   Cook time:_______   Servings:_______

Ingredients

Directions

Notes

Recipe:

Prep time:_______ **Cook time:**_______ **Servings:**_______

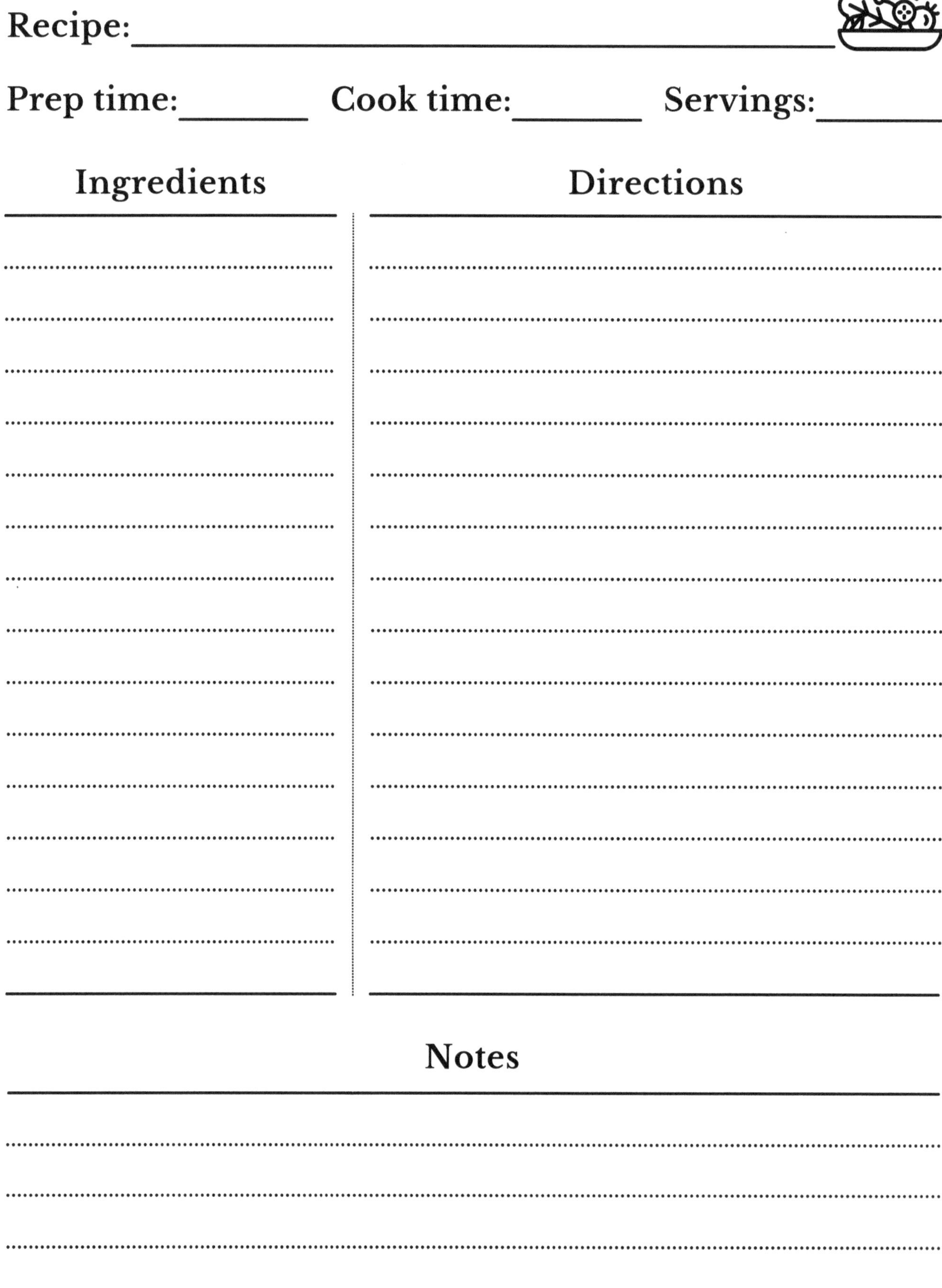

Ingredients | Directions

Notes

Recipe:____

Prep time:________   Cook time:________   Servings:________

Ingredients

Directions

Notes

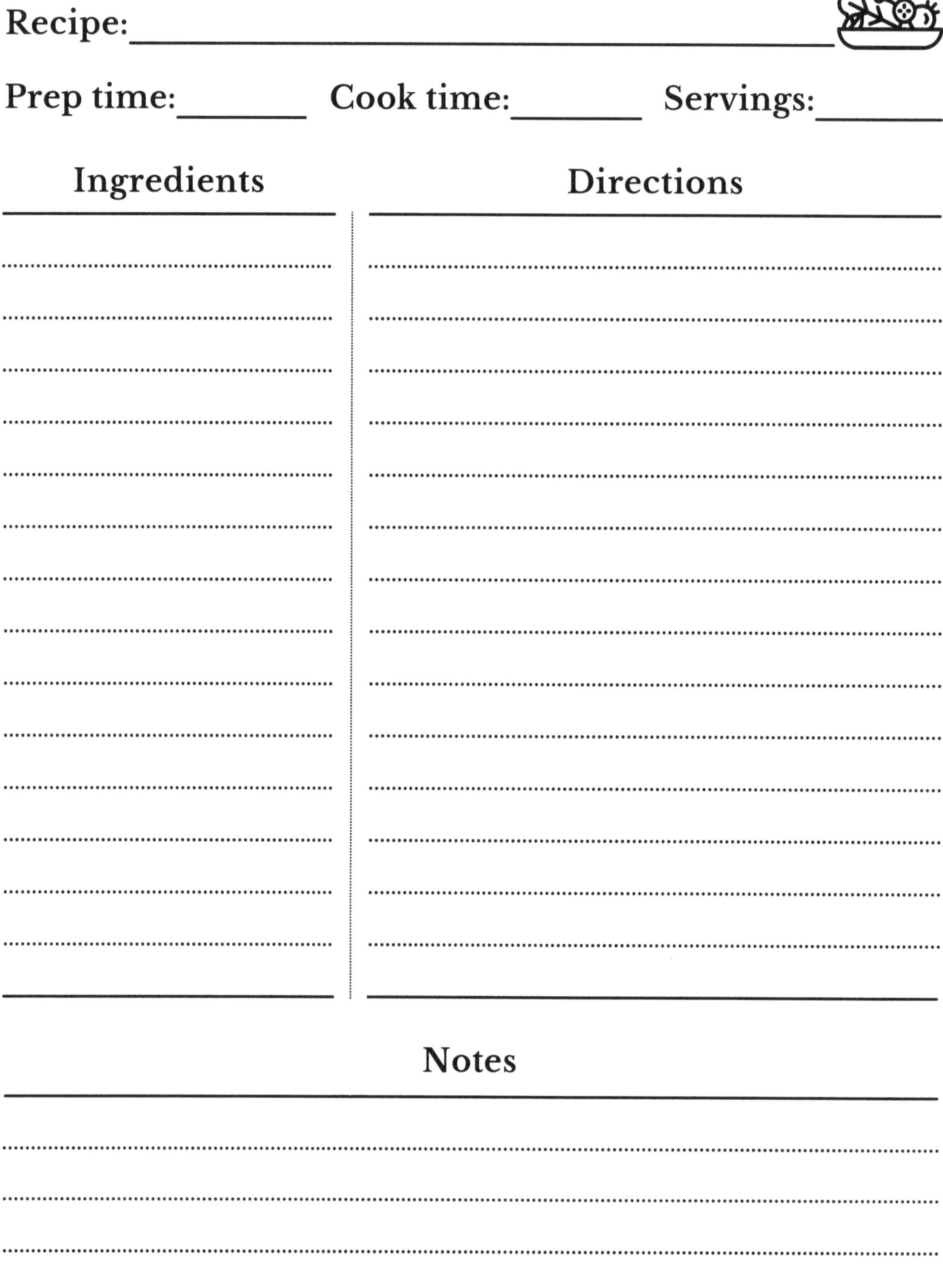

Recipe:

Prep time: ______ Cook time: ______ Servings: ______

Ingredients

Directions

Notes

Recipe:____

Prep time:_______   Cook time:_______   Servings:_______

Ingredients

Directions

Notes

Recipe:____

Prep time:________   Cook time:________   Servings:________

Ingredients

Directions

Notes

Recipe:

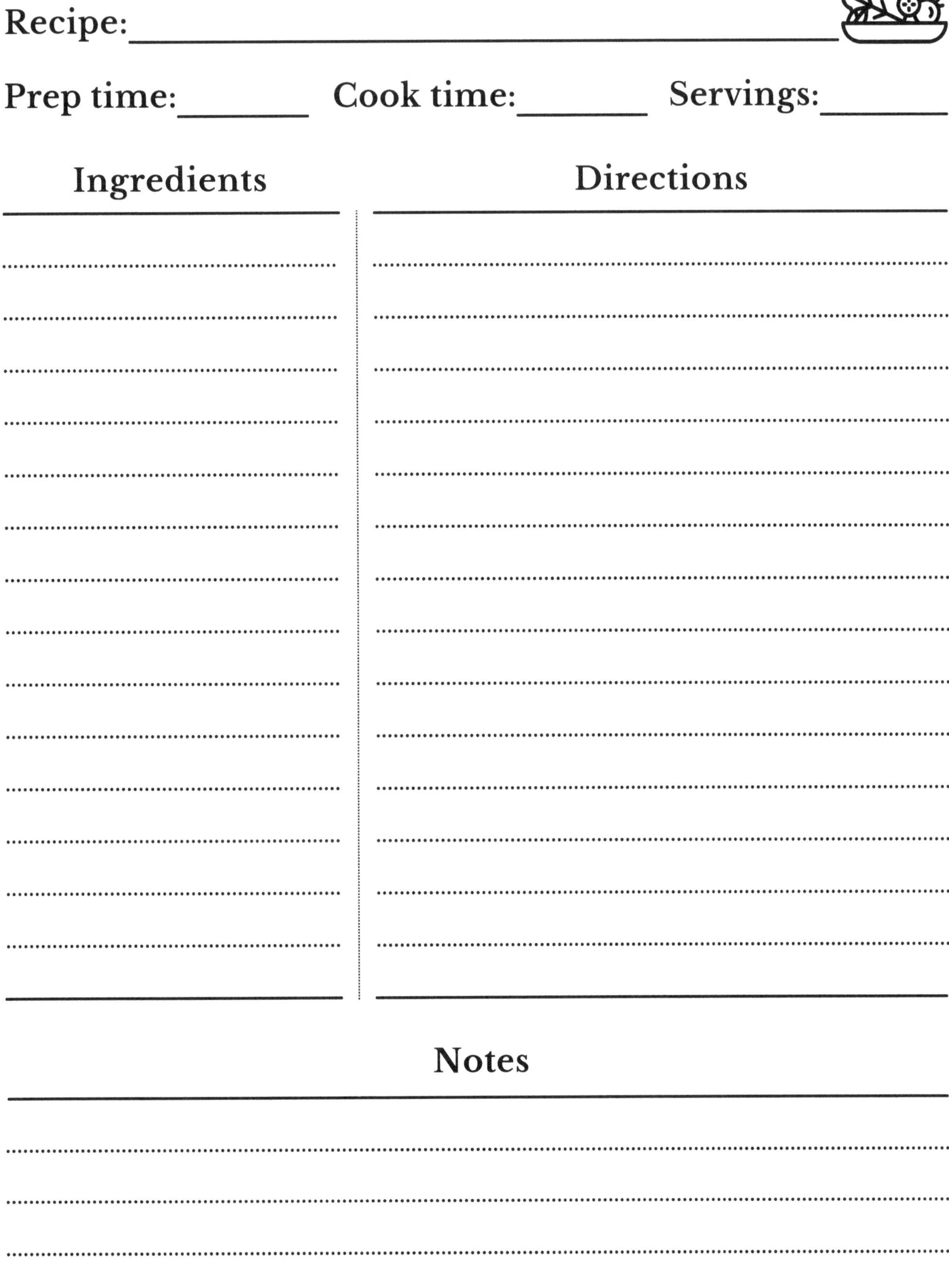

Prep time: ________   **Cook time:** ________   **Servings:** ________

Ingredients

Directions

Notes

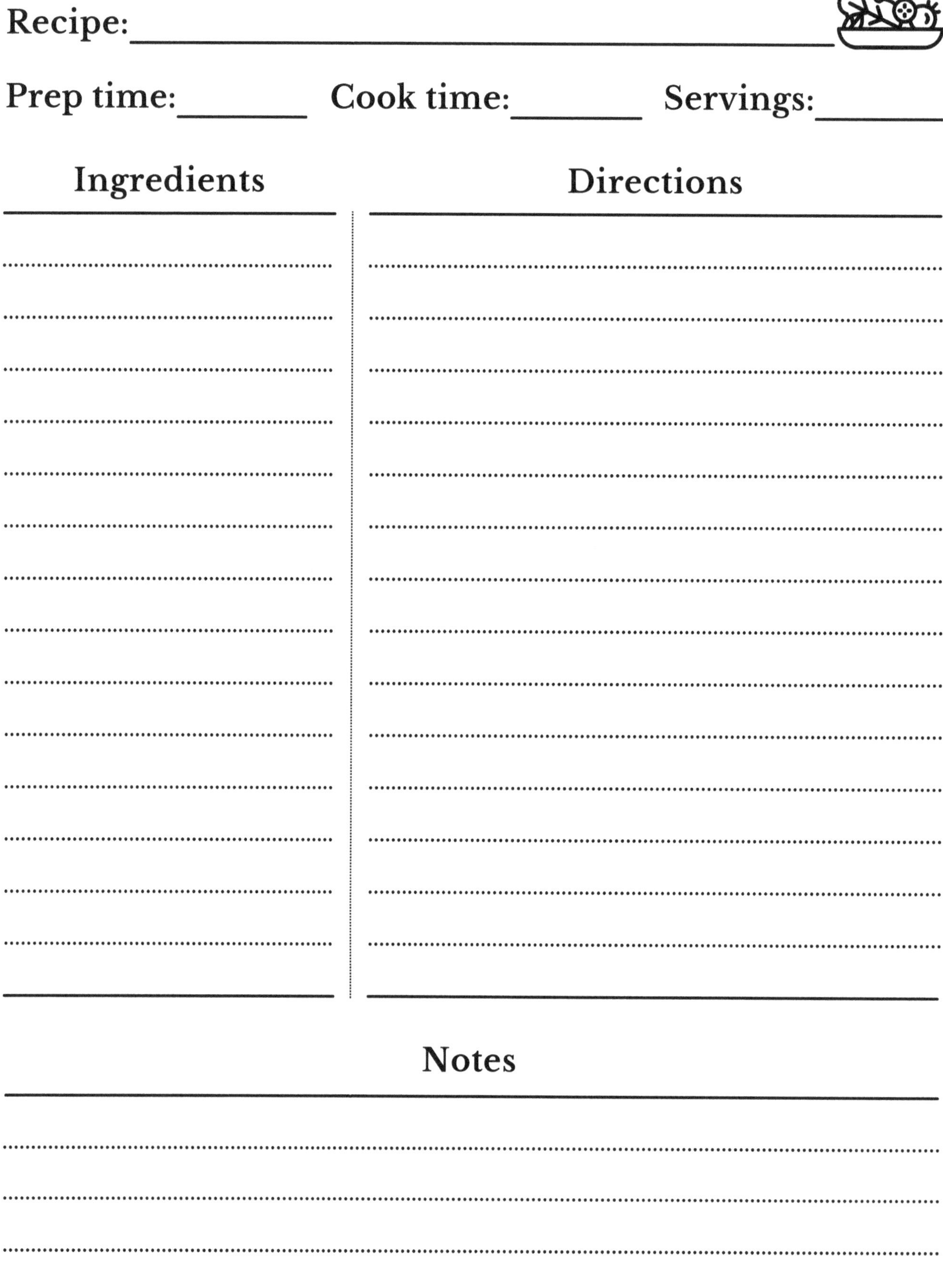

Recipe:____

Prep time:________ Cook time:________ Servings:________

Ingredients

Directions

Notes

Recipe:

Prep time: ______   **Cook time:** ______   **Servings:** ______

Ingredients

Directions

Notes

Recipe:_______________________________________

Prep time:________   Cook time:________   Servings:________

Ingredients

Directions

Notes

Recipe:_______________________________ 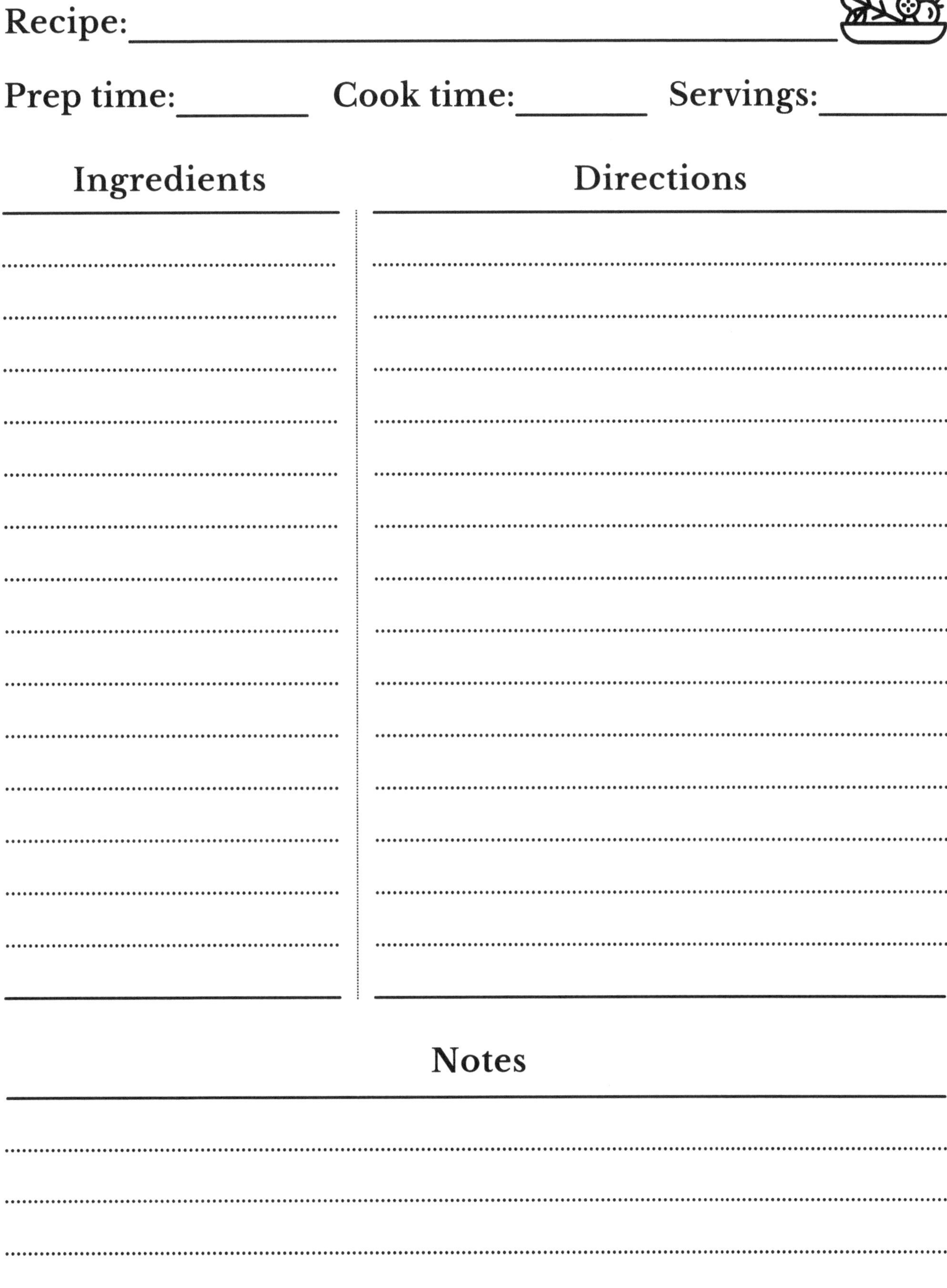

Prep time:________ Cook time:________ Servings:________

Ingredients

Directions

Notes

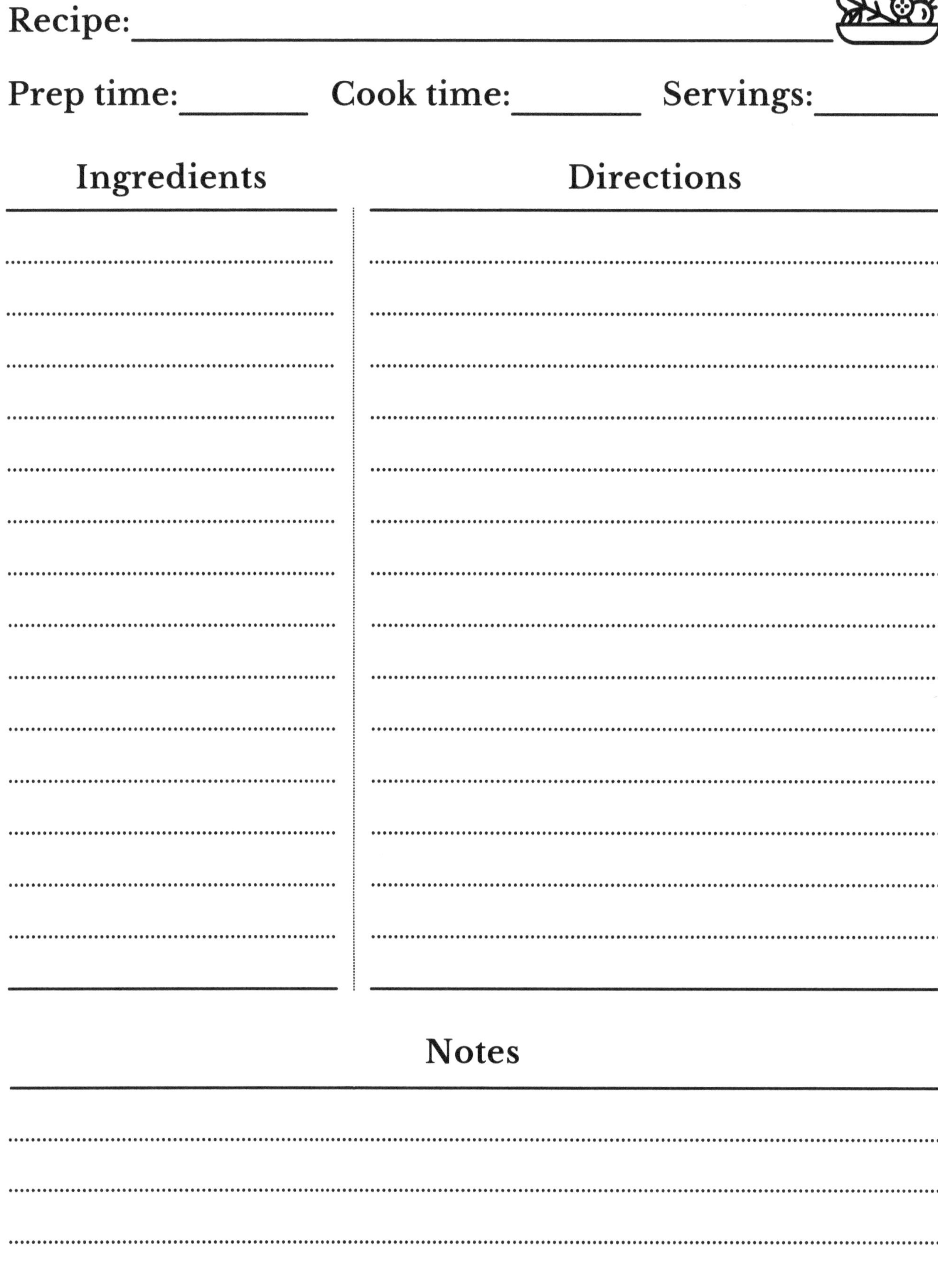

Recipe: ____

Prep time: ________ **Cook time:** ________ **Servings:** ________

Ingredients

Directions

Notes

Recipe:

Prep time:＿＿＿＿＿ Cook time:＿＿＿＿＿ Servings:＿＿＿＿＿

Ingredients

Directions

Notes

Recipe:______________________________________

Prep time:________ Cook time:________ Servings:________

Ingredients

Directions

Notes

Recipe: ________________________________ 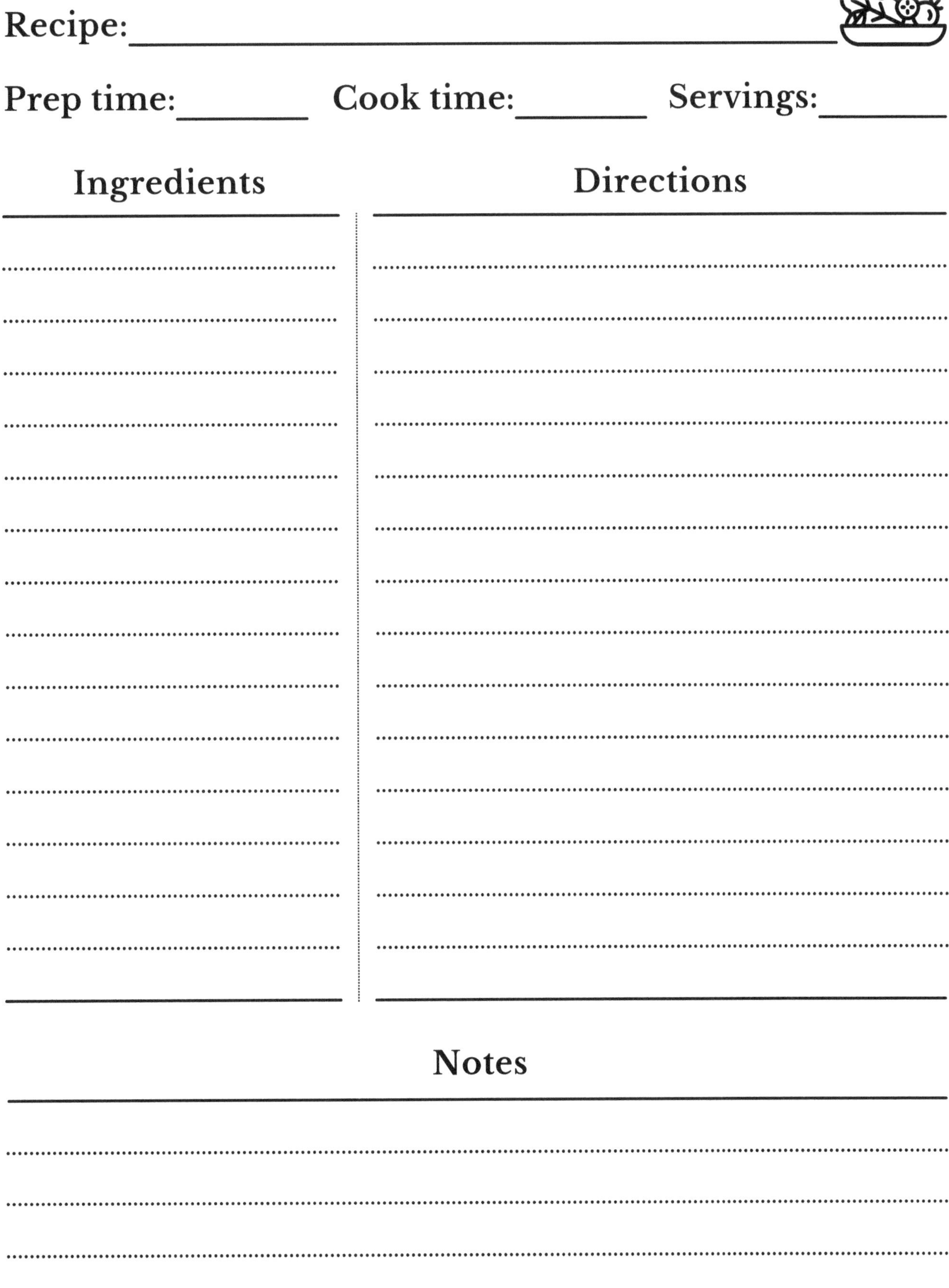

Prep time: _______ **Cook time:** _______ **Servings:** _______

Ingredients | Directions

Notes

Recipe:_______________________________________

Prep time:________ Cook time:________ Servings:________

Ingredients

Directions

Notes

Recipe:

Prep time: ______ **Cook time:** ______ **Servings:** ______

Ingredients

Directions

Notes

Recipe:____

Prep time:________   Cook time:________   Servings:________

Ingredients	Directions

Notes

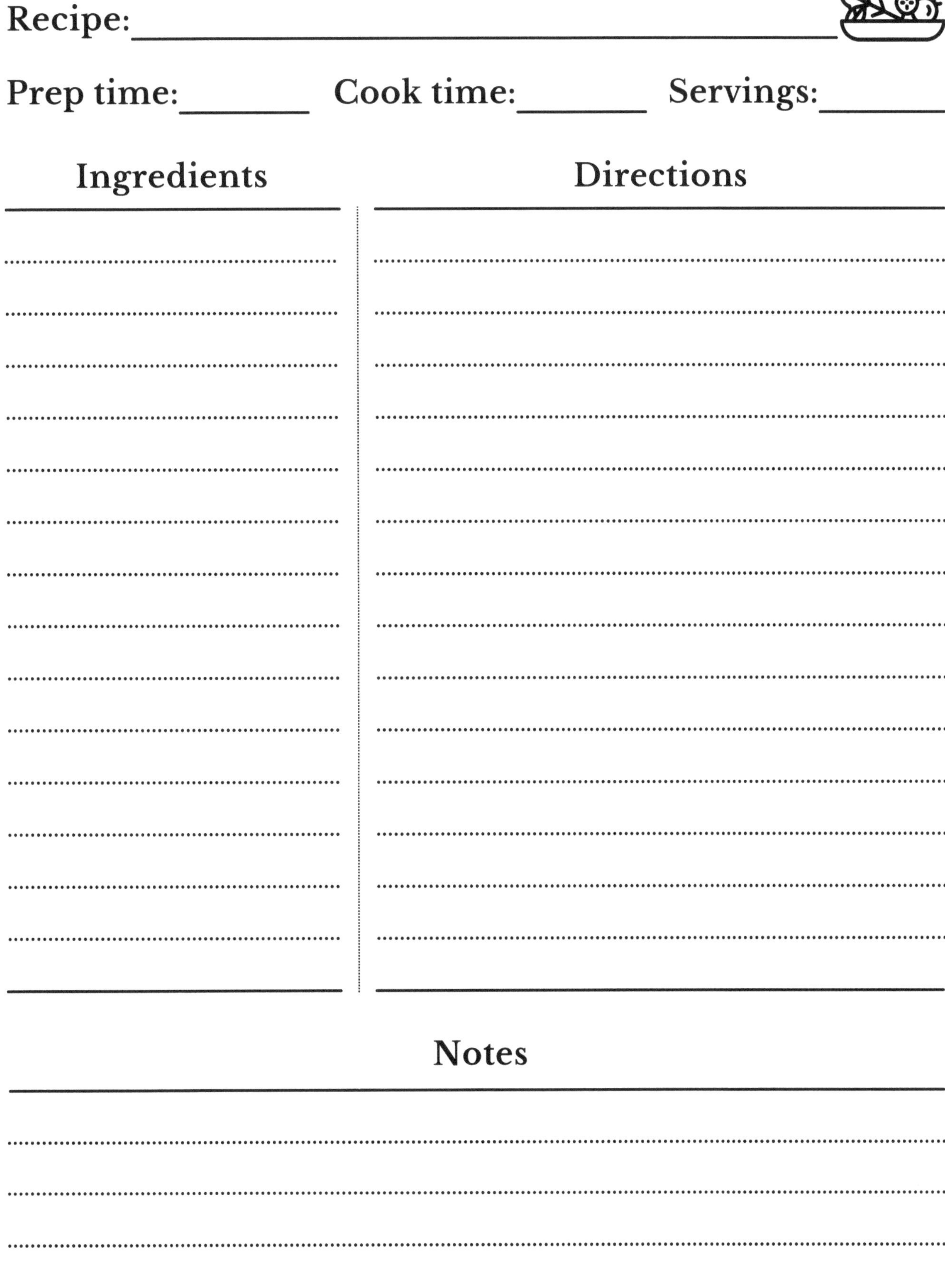

Recipe:____

Prep time:________ Cook time:________ Servings:________

Ingredients

Directions

Notes

Recipe:_______________________________________ 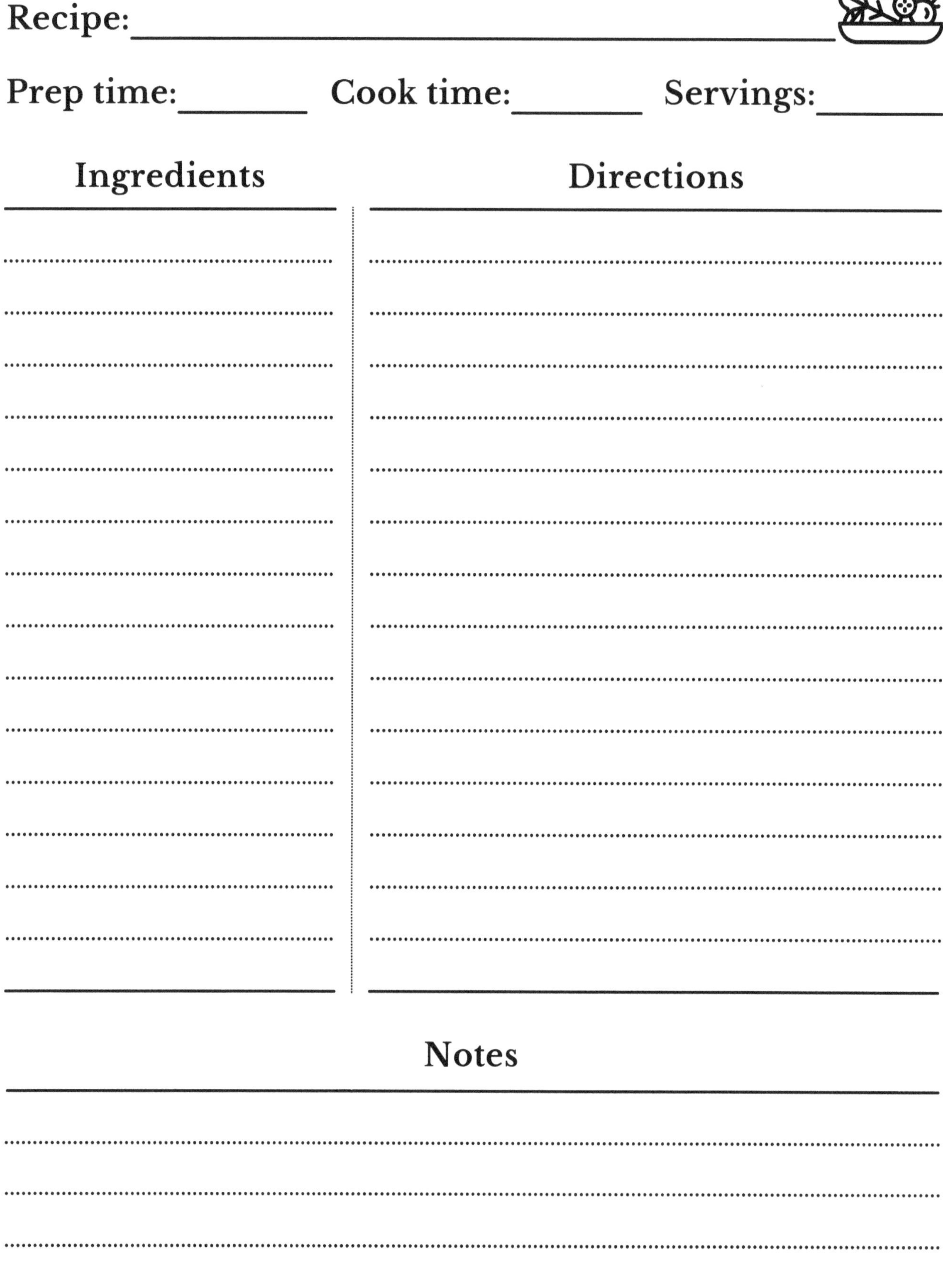

Prep time:_______   Cook time:_______   Servings:_______

Ingredients

Directions

Notes

Recipe:_______________________________________

Prep time:_______   Cook time:_______   Servings:_______

Ingredients

Directions

Notes

Recipe:_______________________________

Prep time: _______   **Cook time:** _______   **Servings:** _______

Ingredients

Directions

Notes

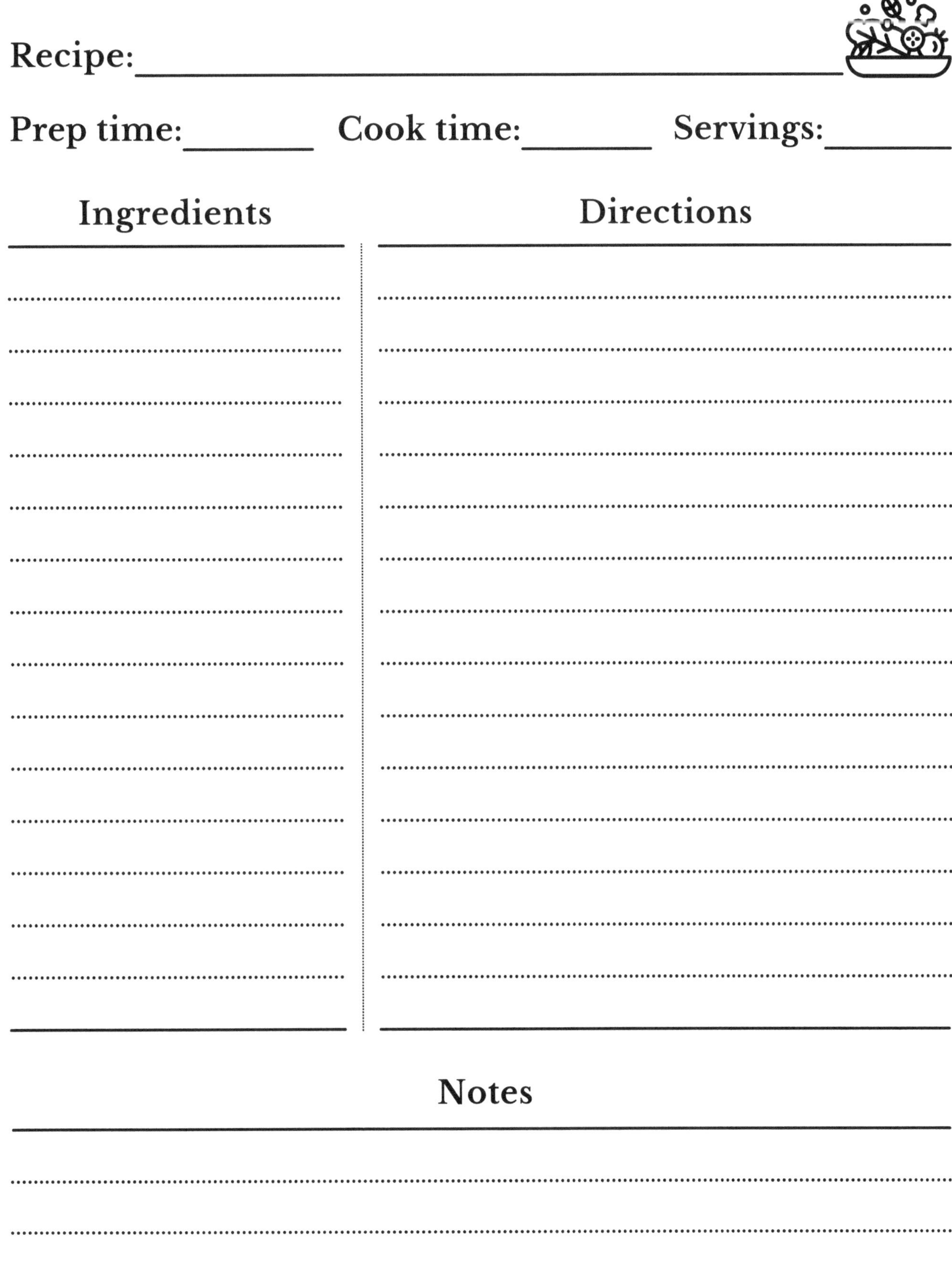

Recipe:____

Prep time:________ Cook time:________ Servings:________

Ingredients

Directions

Notes

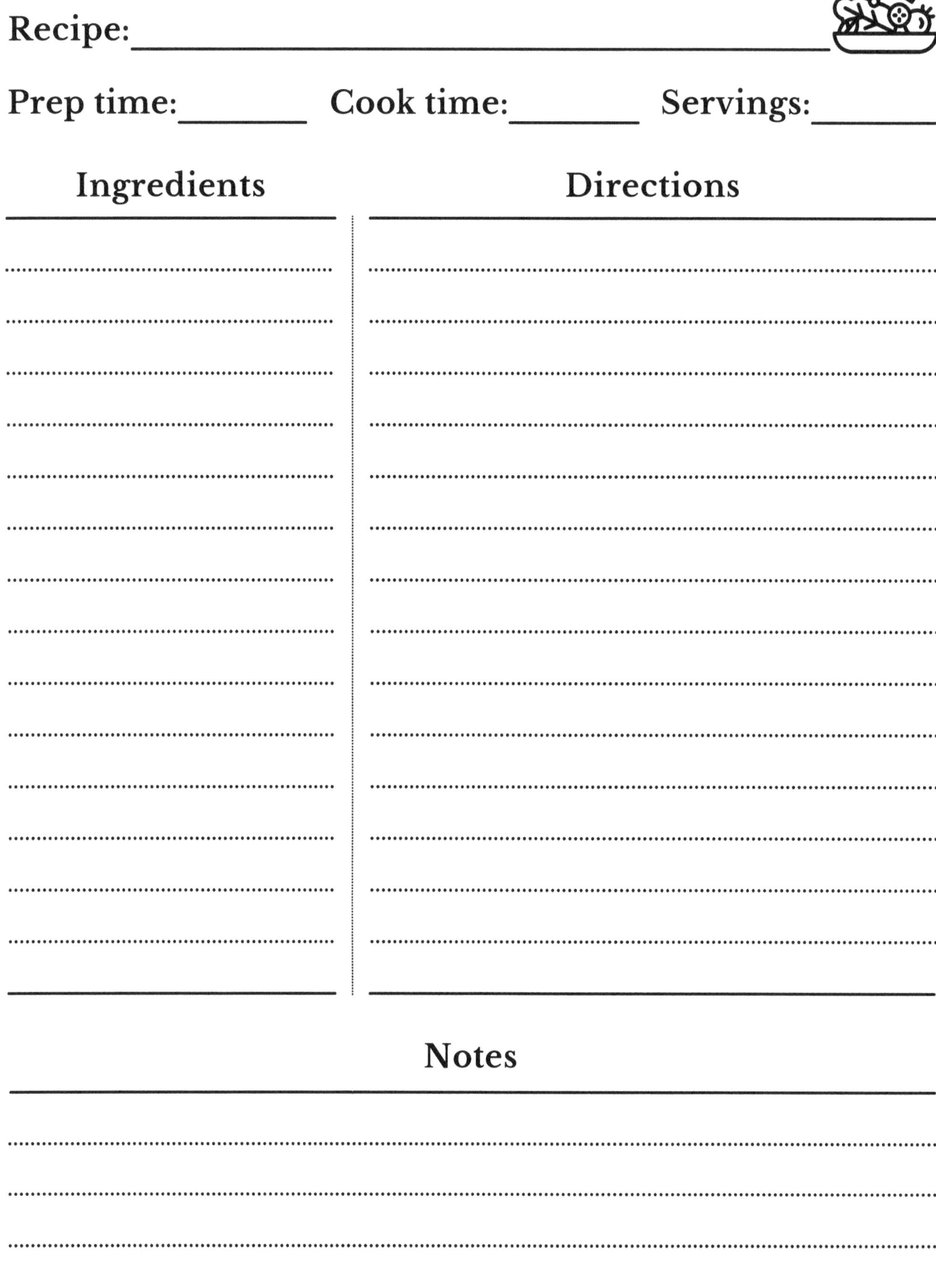

Recipe:____

Prep time:_______ Cook time:_______ Servings:_______

Ingredients

Directions

Notes

Recipe:

Prep time:_______ Cook time:_______ Servings:_______

Ingredients

Directions

Notes

Recipe:___________________________

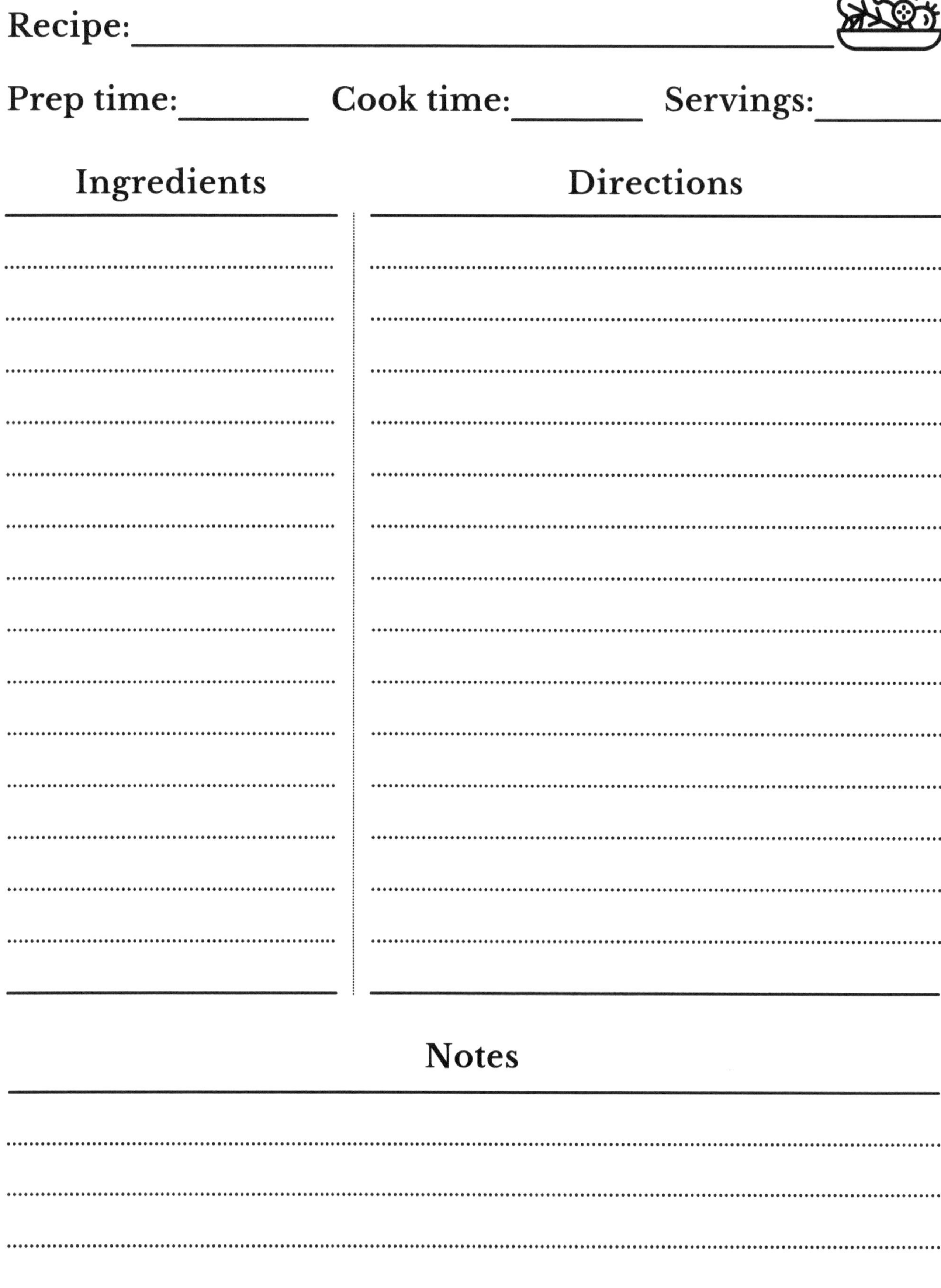

Prep time:________ **Cook time:**________ **Servings:**________

Ingredients	Directions

Notes

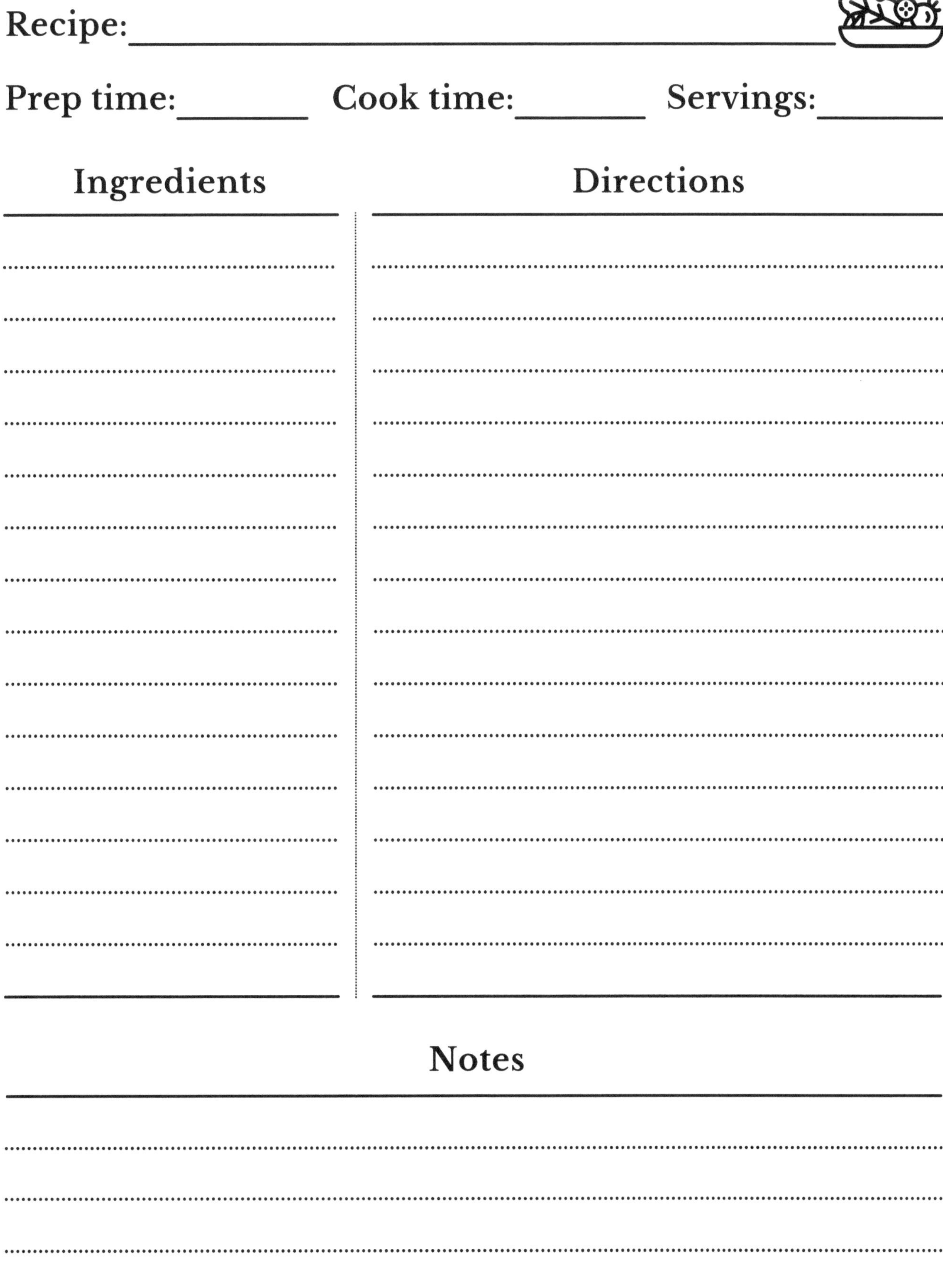

Recipe:____

Prep time:________ Cook time:________ Servings:________

Ingredients

Directions

Notes

Recipe:

Prep time: _______ Cook time: _______ Servings: _______

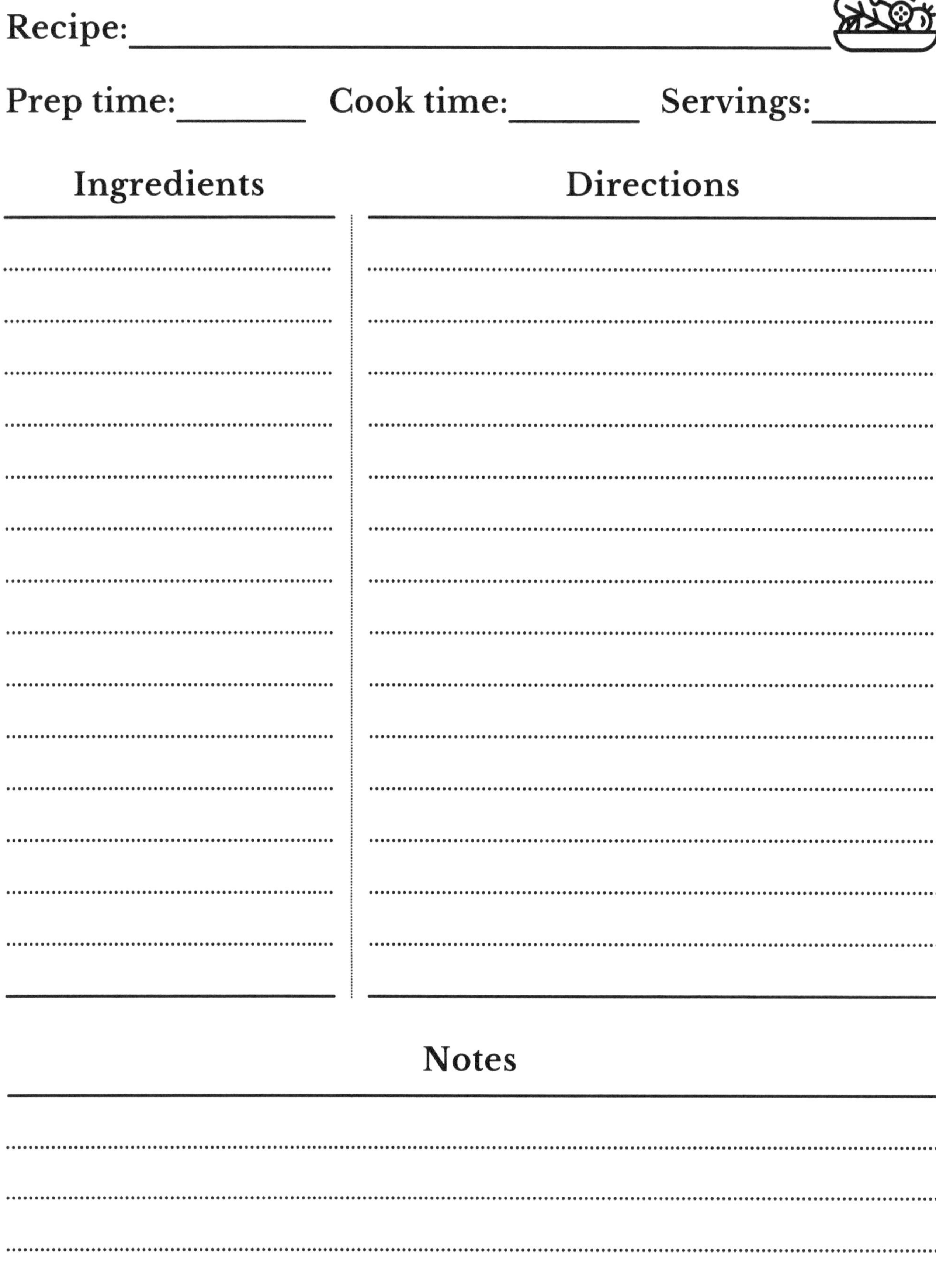

Ingredients

Directions

Notes

Recipe:____

Prep time:________   Cook time:________   Servings:________

Ingredients

Directions

Notes

Recipe:

Prep time: **Cook time:** **Servings:**

Ingredients

Directions

Notes

Recipe:____

Prep time:________   Cook time:________   Servings:________

Ingredients

Directions

Notes

Recipe:

Prep time:_______ Cook time:_______ Servings:_______

Ingredients

Directions

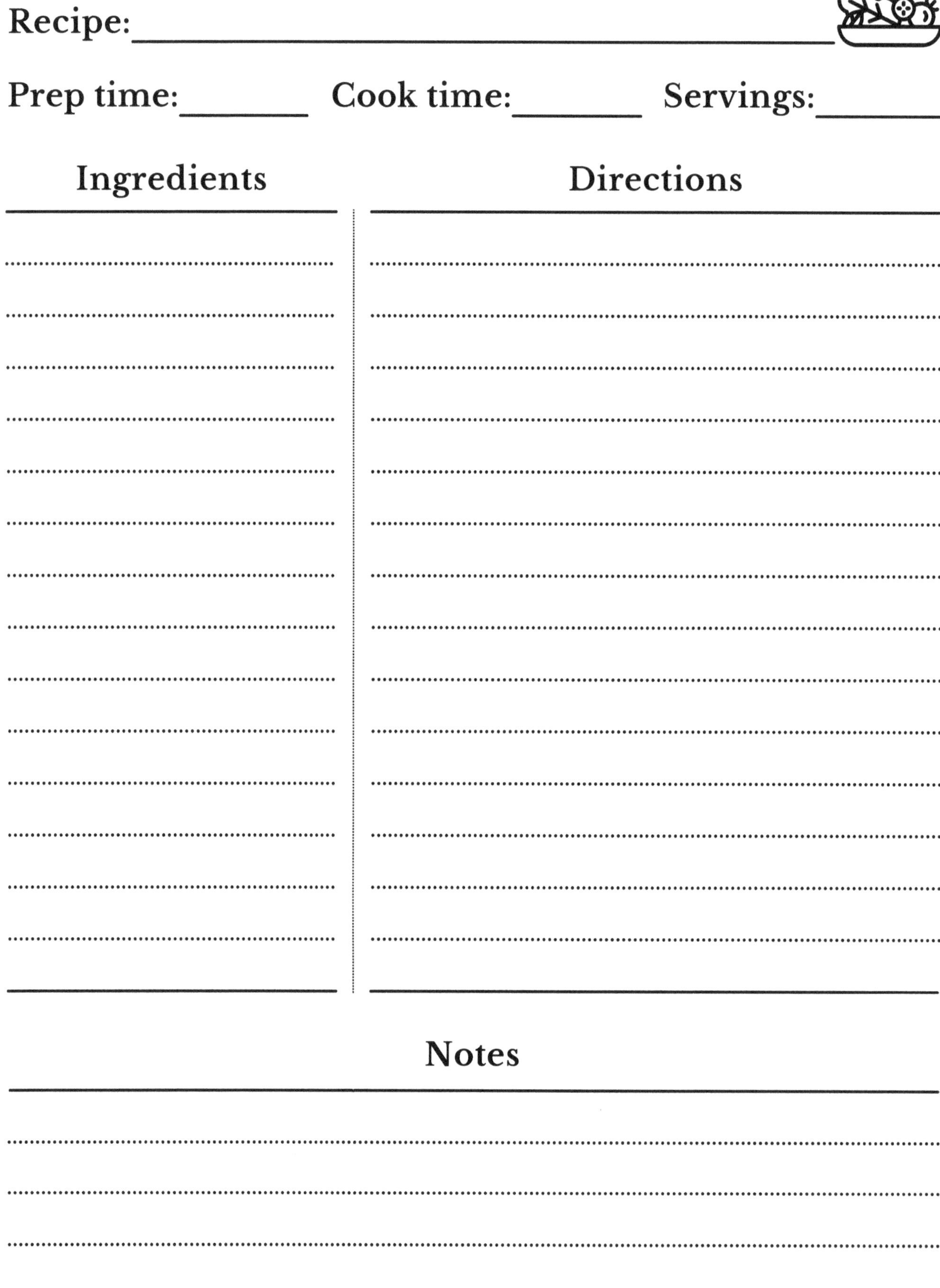

Notes

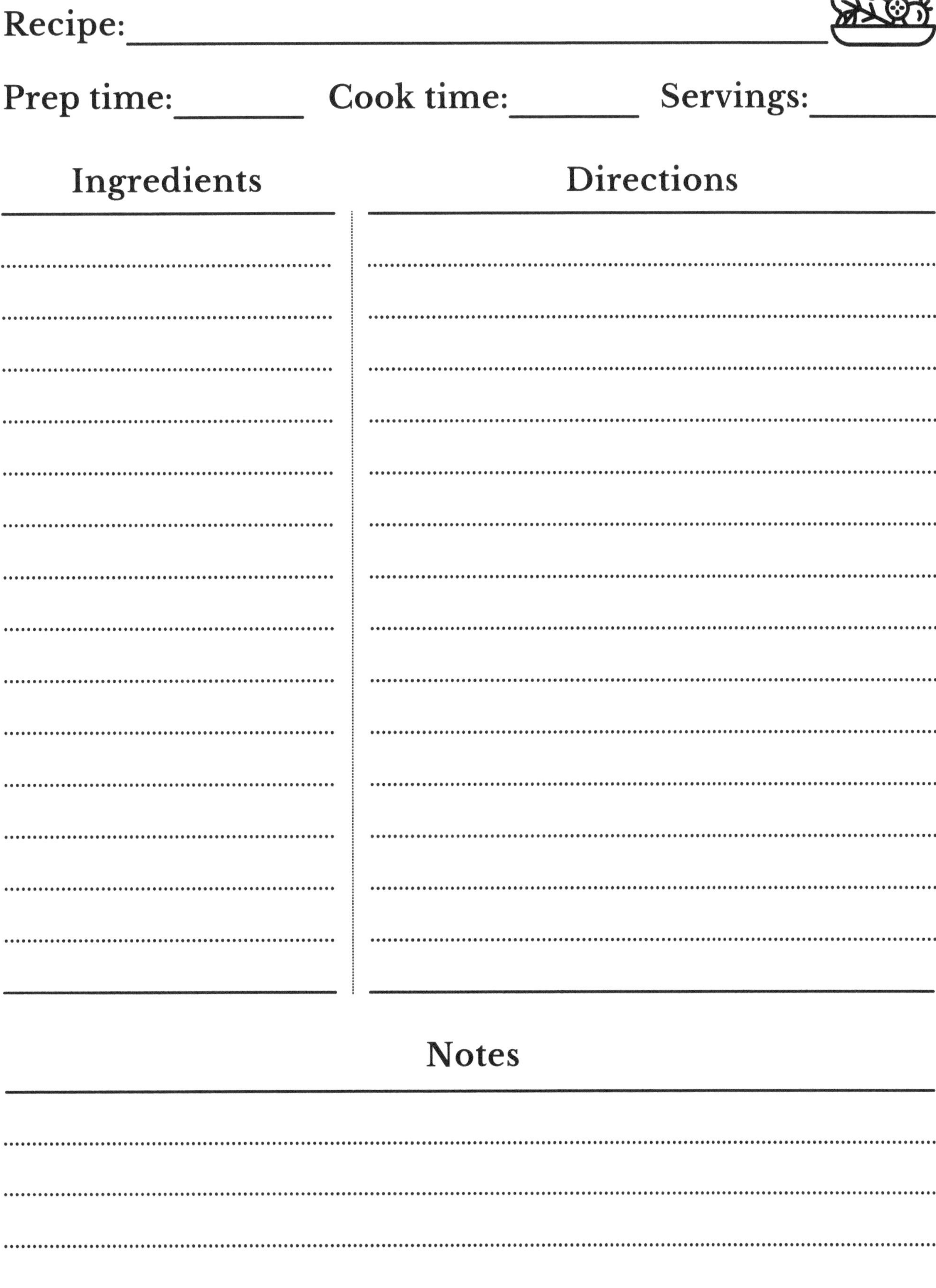

Recipe:____

Prep time:________   Cook time:________   Servings:________

Ingredients

Directions

Notes

Recipe:

Prep time: ______ Cook time: ______ Servings: ______

Ingredients

Directions

Notes

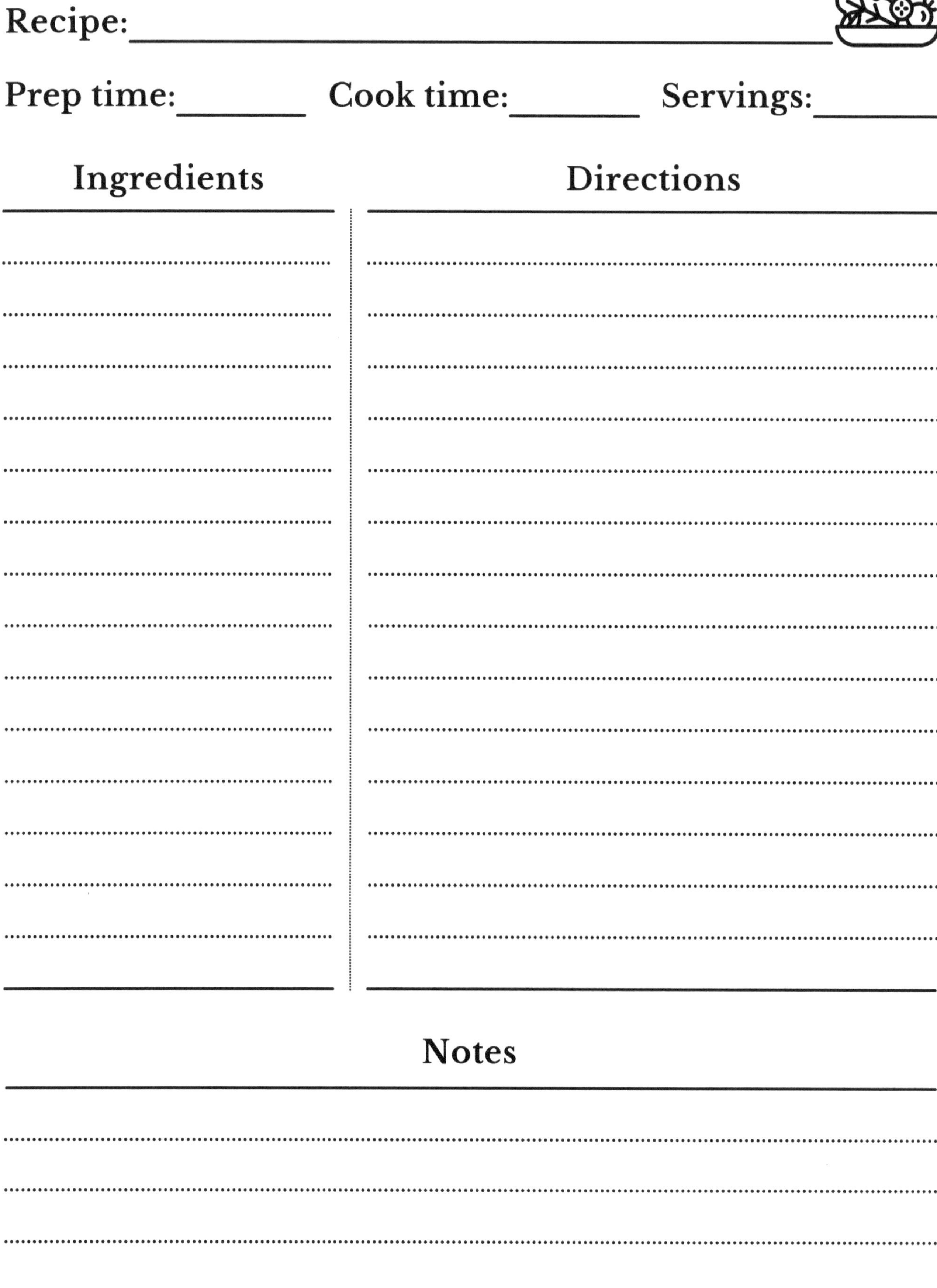

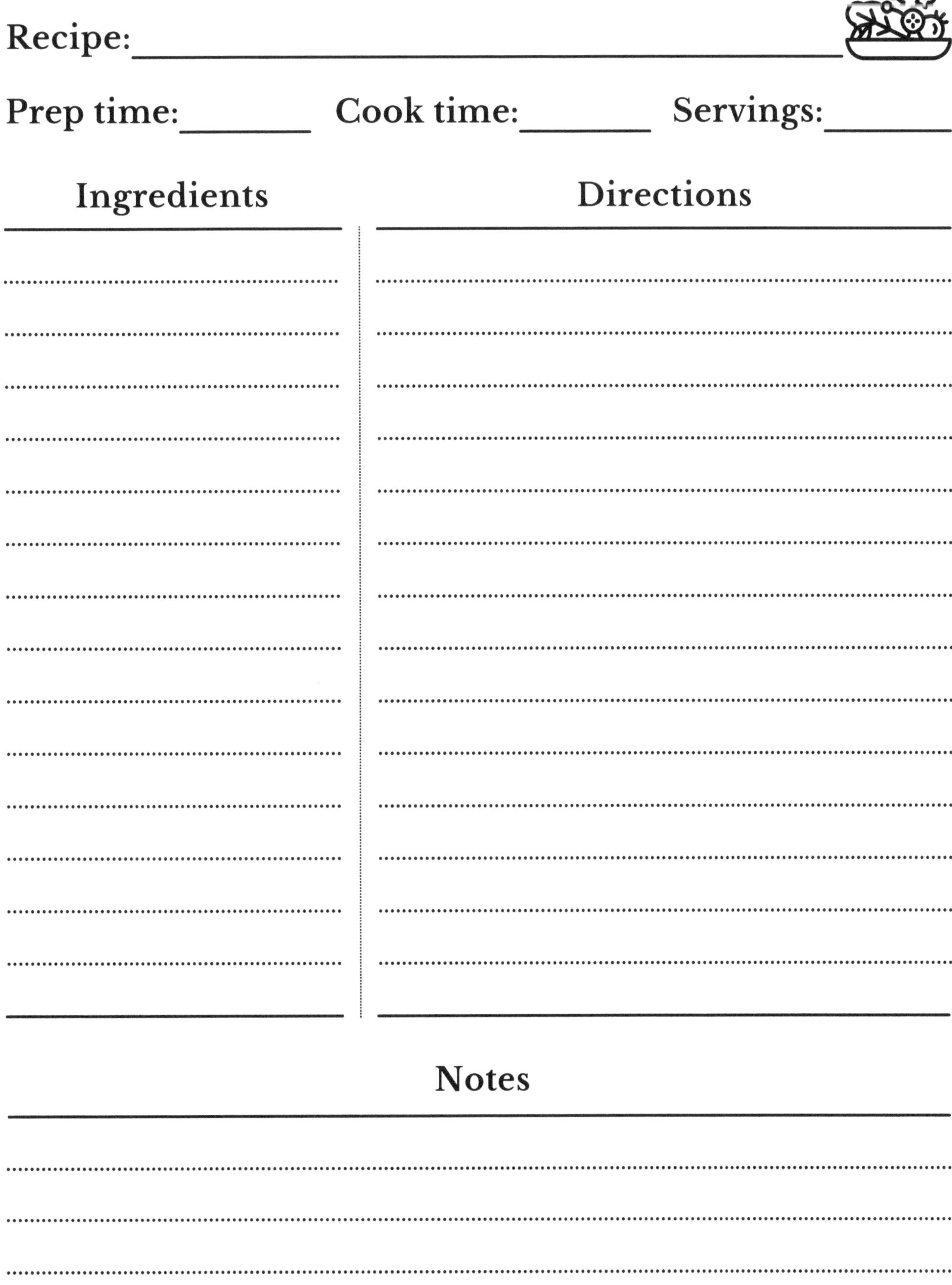

Recipe:____

Prep time:________   Cook time:________   Servings:________

Ingredients

Directions

Notes

Recipe:

Prep time: _______ Cook time: _______ Servings: _______

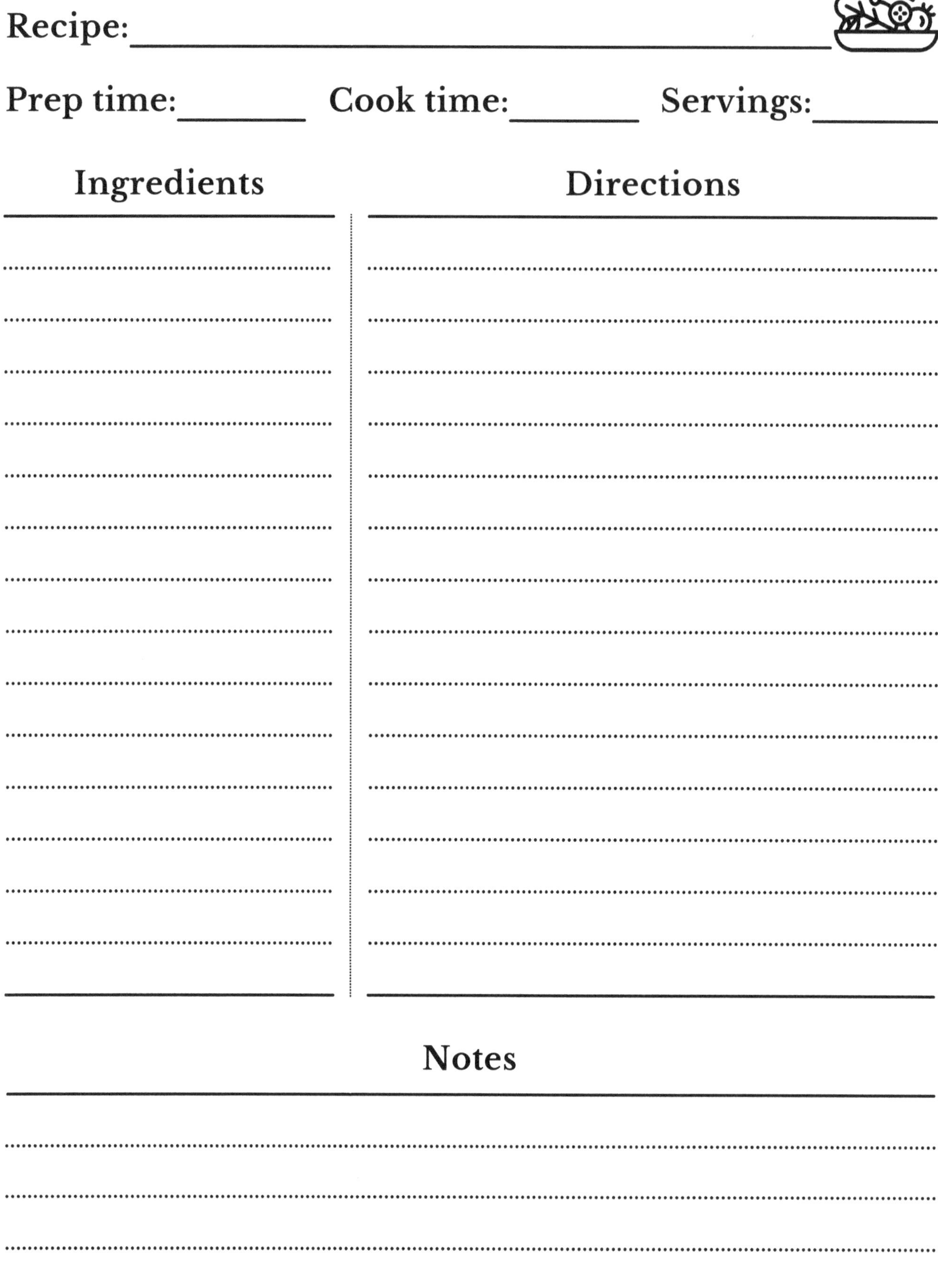

Ingredients

Directions

Notes

Recipe:____

Prep time:_______   Cook time:_______   Servings:_______

Ingredients

Directions

Notes

Recipe:

Prep time: _______ **Cook time:** _______ **Servings:** _______

Ingredients

Directions

Notes

Recipe:_______________________________________

Prep time:________   Cook time:________   Servings:________

Ingredients

Directions

Notes

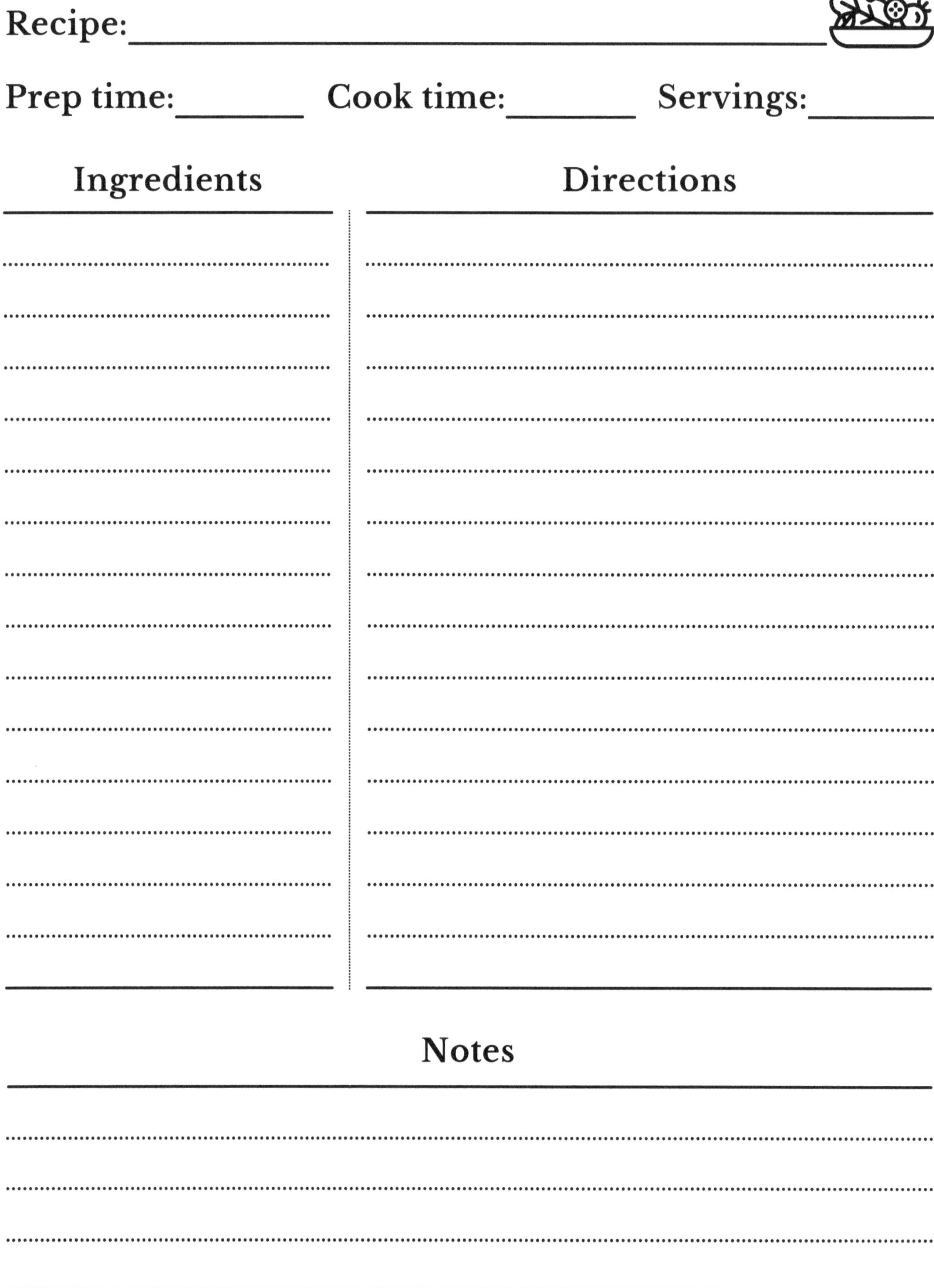

Recipe: ___________________________________

Prep time: ________ **Cook time:** ________ **Servings:** ________

Ingredients

Directions

Notes

Recipe:____

Prep time:________ Cook time:________ Servings:________

Ingredients

Directions

Notes

Recipe:_______________________________________

Prep time:________   Cook time:________   Servings:________

Ingredients

Directions

Notes

Recipe:_______________________________________

Prep time:________   Cook time:________   Servings:________

Ingredients

Directions

Notes

Recipe:_________________________________

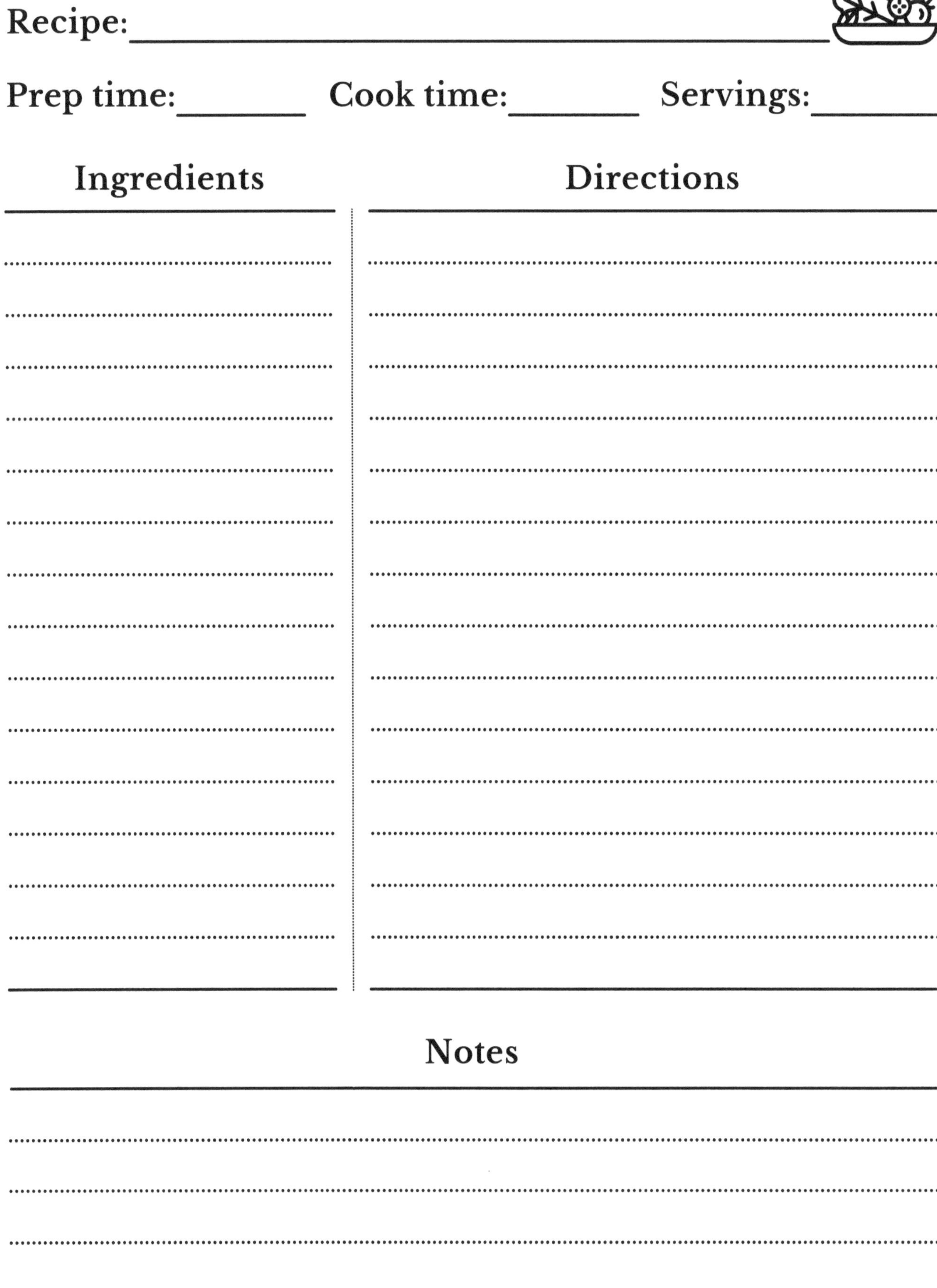

Prep time:_______ **Cook time:**_______ **Servings:**_______

Ingredients | Directions

Notes

Recipe:____

Prep time:________   Cook time:________   Servings:________

Ingredients

Directions

Notes

Recipe:____

Prep time:_________ Cook time:_________ Servings:_________

Ingredients	Directions

Notes

Recipe:

Prep time: _______ **Cook time:** _______ **Servings:** _______

Ingredients | Directions

Notes

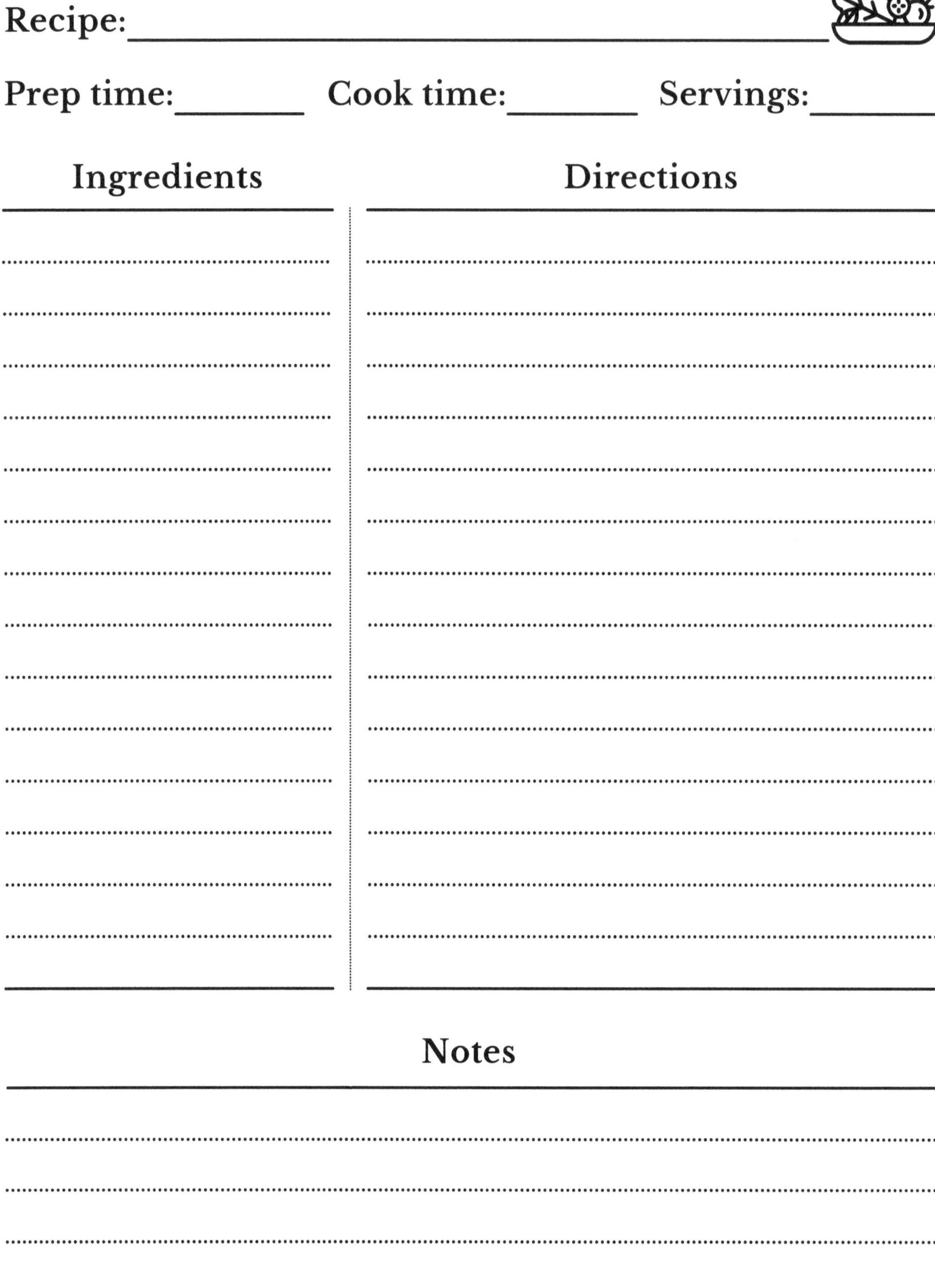

Recipe:____

Prep time:________ **Cook time:**________ **Servings:**________

Ingredients

Directions

Notes

Recipe:_______________________________________

Prep time:_______ Cook time:_______ Servings:_______

Ingredients	Directions

Notes

Recipe:

Prep time: ______   **Cook time:** ______   **Servings:** ______

Ingredients

Directions

Notes

Recipe:

Prep time: _______   Cook time: _______   Servings: _______

Ingredients

Directions

Notes

Recipe:_______________________________

Prep time:______ **Cook time:**______ **Servings:**______

Ingredients | Directions

Notes

Recipe:____

Prep time:________   Cook time:________   Servings:________

Ingredients

Directions

Notes

Prep time:_______ Cook time:_______ Servings:_______

Ingredients

Directions

Notes